Heart to Heart

*Encouragement from a
Christian Homeschool Mom*

Heart to Heart

*Encouragement from a
Christian Homeschool Mom*

Vicki Lewis

Heart to Heart

Encouragement from a Christian Homeschool Mom

Vicki Lewis

Welcome! I invite you to grab a cup of coffee (or tea) and come sit with me at my kitchen table.

The most important thing to know about me is that I am a believer in the Lord Jesus Christ. Having been a Bible study teacher for many years, my heart desires to live a life that is centered on Jesus and to demonstrate to women what it looks like to follow Jesus Christ faithfully.

I wrote this book originally because I wanted to share some of the lessons the Lord had taught me over more than twenty years of being a wife, a mother, and a home-schooling parent. Blessed with the opportunity to update that book, contribute encouragement articles to several home schooling publications, and create a blog online, this is a collection of some of my favorite devotions. There are fifty-two devotions: one for each week of the year.

I also wanted to leave a written legacy to our children and grandchildren so that they might know why we made some of the choices we did for our family.

Anything good or worthwhile in my life and ministry is totally due to the Lord Jesus Christ. He taught me what was most important in my original career choice of education. He brought me my dearest companion and husband, Steve. He gave us four dear children to raise for Him. He strengthened my resolve to complete what we started in home schooling. He encouraged me whenever I felt like giving up. He brought other godly women alongside to inspire and sharpen me, to rejoice with me, and cry with me.

To the precious mother who reads this book, I hope you know how much the Lord desires to walk with you daily through every moment of your life. He wants you to have a personal relationship with Him, one in which you surrender to Him and His loving plan for your life and the lives of your family. I hope that all of us as homeschooling mothers would continually have soft, teachable spirits and that we would grow in grace and the knowledge of the Lord Jesus Christ (2 Peter 3:18).

Are you interested in a fresh and relevant study of the Bible, the kind that blows the dust off your Bible and the cobwebs out of the corners of your mind? A study of what the Bible teaches us women about devotion and passion and joy? I am!

Do you have that cup of coffee? Please come sit with me...and bring your Bible!

Beside Quiet Waters

Our family had just returned from vacation at a rented cabin in the Colorado mountains situated by a peaceful stream. Vacation meant time for the two women of our home to sleep, read, nap, read, rest, and—did I mention read?

The four men in my life fished patiently in a nearby pond, usually barefoot and carefree. By August, the trout remaining in that stocked pond were wise to the ways of young fishermen and refused to fall for the salmon-eggs-on-a-hook trick.

Life was simpler. Meals were pre-planned and easy. Family devotions occurred at some meal. Chores were assigned in teams and rotated. Evenings were filled with games, laughing, singing, and reading aloud as the darkness softly wrapped around us.

And always the presence of the stream making a soothing sound that mingled with the movement of the wind through the aspens, making me think of the verse from Psalm 23 that says, "He leads me beside quiet waters."

Now we are home and I am back to my non-vacation world of responsibilities. We are starting school in two weeks and I am nearly ready. Do I need to order more books? The garden is still not weeded after all this time and now the weeds are starting to look like part of the design! My shoulders begin to tense up around my ears like earmuffs. The tranquil sound of the river is fading in my memory.

As we begin a new year of home schooling, I simply do not want to forget the sound of the river and the peace it brings. Dear Lord, I pray, how can I retain the peacefulness of that cabin by the river in my everyday life?

And He gently speaks to my spirit, reminding me that peace is not a place, but it is His blessing on our family because of our relationships with Him. He has made peace readily available and I just have to appropriate it.

"All your children will be taught by the LORD, and great will be their peace" (Isaiah 54:13). Yes, Lord, please be the teacher of our precious children this year! I commit each one into Your capable hands. I promise to order books, list daily pages that need to be accomplished, and correct writing assignments. But I humbly ask You to be in charge of our home school this year.

Teach us more about who You are, help us to see Your hand working in our lives, and cause each of us to grow in faith, character, and knowledge this coming year. As a result, may each of our children also experience Your peace.

"You will keep in perfect peace [the homeschooling mother] whose mind is steadfast, because [she] trusts in You" (Isaiah 26:3).

I ask this for myself, Lord. I have trusted You with my salvation and my life, so I trust You now with all the details of a new school year—especially my attitudes, Lord. I take hold of You and lean heavily upon You. Thank You, in advance, for what You will accomplish this year.

The tenseness in my shoulders eases. Taking a deep breath, I slowly exhale. Okay, Lord, I am ready for the adventure of this year, I pray, promising to walk hand in hand with Him daily. And somehow the sound of that Rocky Mountain river seems more noticeable!

What are Your Reasons for Home Schooling?

When we began home schooling, Steve and I wrote a list of reasons why we wanted to do this. And not just a few—we wanted reasons from many different areas of life. So every time we read or heard something that made us think, "Yes! That's why we're doing this," we copied it down.

Eventually we realized that our list could be grouped into several categories. Some of the items on the list were academic benefits, some were spiritual, and others were related to character training, social training, or benefitted the family as a whole.

We now have a list that has been modified, matured, and polished after many years of home schooling. We have shared this at home school seminars, telling beginners how important it is to know why they have chosen to home school.

It helps to have considered this before someone (like your mother-in-law!) asks, "What do you think you are doing?" Also, on those days when you yourself wonder why you're doing this, rereading your list reminds you of what really matters. Suppose math is not going well or someone's attitude needs major reconstructive surgery—looking through a list of compelling reasons to persevere puts things in perspective.

Our personal, primary reason for home schooling is to be good stewards of the precious children that God has given us. To do anything else would be, for us, direct disobedience. Since we believe that God has called us to home school, we trust Him to supply all we need to accomplish that.

Here are some of our spiritual reasons for home schooling:

1. It enables us as parents to fulfill our responsibility to God to bring up our children "in the training and instruction of the Lord" (Ephesians 6:4).

2. It enables us to limit our childrens' exposure to a secular worldview.

3. We are able to design an education that gives God all the respect and honor He is due.

4. Daily, we can encourage our children to have and maintain a personal relationship with Jesus Christ.

5. We have the opportunity to disciple our children in the Christian faith and to equip the next generation to disciple their own children. Home schooling is a multigenerational vision.

Developing character was another family value that we considered important. Home schooling gives us plenty of opportunities, in addition to regular family life, to practice developing Christ-like behavior. Some of the character benefits we found include:

1. We can demonstrate to our children what the qualities of commitment, perseverance, and obedience look like as we daily obey the Lord in home schooling, parenting, and through our marriage.

2. Both parents and children can emphasize and practice Christ-like character in daily situations.

3. Our children can be grounded in God's love for them and our love. They can be assured that they are unique and "fearfully and wonderfully made" (Psalm 139:14).

4. We have all day, every day, to allow our children to develop godly wisdom in their decisions.

5. Our children can learn to stand alone for God's truth.

6. Our children can understand the various relationships in which they have been placed. How does God want a son to be Christ-like? A daughter? A father and a mother? As a family, how can we grow together as brothers and sisters in the Lord?

We also came up with a list of academic reasons promoting home schooling, including the following:

1. We have the privilege of choosing and implementing the entire curriculum.

2. We are able to integrate a Christian worldview into all school subjects, allowing us to identify and discuss other non-Christian worldviews and practice discernment.

3. The tutorial method (teaching one-on-one) is a superior method of education, allowing us to individualize each subject to each child.

4. Less instructional time is required.

5. We are able to design our own yearly, weekly, and daily schedules, giving us much more flexibility than families constrained by a traditional school schedule.

There were also a number of social benefits of home schooling for which we are grateful:

1. Our children have close, consistent contact with adult role models. ("Walk with the wise and become wise, for a companion of fools suffers harm," Proverbs 13:20.)
2. We can help them develop confident and independent thinking away from negative peer pressure.
3. A home setting offers increased protection from false philosophies and immoral temptations.
4. All our learning takes place in an age-integrated setting.
5. We have time for family ministry and hospitality.
6. Positive socialization—beyond just playing nicely together in the sandbox—involves learning how to have an intelligent conversation with someone of any age, how to yield or defer, how to be self-controlled, how to be well-behaved in various situations, how to resolve conflict, how to stay married, how to be parents, and much more.

Lastly, we have the category of family benefits. In a time when the concept of family is disintegrating and the enemy of our souls is on the prowl, we desire to do everything humanly possible to strengthen our family. Through home schooling:

1. We have the quality and quantity of time to develop a unique bond between parent and child.
2. Our children are encouraged to respect parental authority instead of preferring the influence of their peers.
3. Siblings receive daily practice in loving and forgiving each other, which reduces or eliminates sibling rivalry.
4. Our children can work alongside us as we accomplish worthwhile projects together.
5. As parents, we get to relearn the school curriculum from a Christian worldview.

So that's our list! What's yours? Don't have a list yet? Then start today to create one, asking God to remind you of the things that are most important for your family. Know also that your list of reasons may grow or change over time, and that's okay.

"Some goals in life are worthwhile, some are not. The worthwhile ones always require sacrifice. Remembering why I am doing what I am doing is what keeps me going each day."
George Mueller

I Don't Think I Can Do This!

While talking with other homeschooling mothers, I have heard them say, "I don't think I can do this!" or "I feel so inadequate to teach my own children!"

Well, the truth is that we are inadequate! I too have days filled with doubts because I realize that I don't know everything, that I don't have hours and hours to prepare for each school day, and I am not sure how to meet the unique needs of each child. In my own strength and resources, I fall far short of the ideal homeschooling mom that I imagine I should be.

Whenever this happens I inevitably hear the quiet voice of the Lord reminding me that the success of our home schooling does not depend on my eloquence, organization, or abilities. Home schooling is a conviction that He gave Steve and me, a certainty in our hearts that this was the obedient and God-honoring thing to do. God seems to highlight Scripture verses through our family devotion times to remind me just whose reputation is at stake here.

"Commit to the LORD whatever you do, and he will establish your plans" (Proverbs 16:3). Each morning, as a family, we commit our day to God. Having done that, it is now God's responsibility to cause our home schooling to succeed. Does that mean we can quit schooling and just sit back and wait for knowledge to fall into our laps? No, but it does mean that the final outcome of what we do is part of God's plan for us.

God says in His word that He will honor those who honor Him (1 Samuel 2:30). That is one goal that keeps me focused and protected from discouragement. God takes me back to the original spiritual vision that He gave us and reminds me not to question in the dark times of difficulty or doubt what He has shown me in the light.

"In his heart a man plans his course, but the Lord determines his steps" (Proverbs 16:9). Here is that verse paraphrased for home-schooling mothers: "In her heart, a mom considers the day's lesson plans, but the actual day and its events will unfold as God Himself has determined." Relax and take a deep breath, I remind myself. Okay, I promise to plan carefully, Lord, but I will be flexible and yield to Your divine interruptions and changes of plan to our school day.

Because God specifically has asked us to raise our children for Him, He promises to make available to us everything we need in order to do this job. It would be silly of me to expect one of our children to wash the family car if I failed to provide the needed items to accomplish the job, like soap, water, sponges, or towels.

"His divine power has given us everything we need for a godly life through our knowledge of him" (2 Peter 1:3). In the final analysis, this homeschooling lifestyle was begun by God's urging and He promises to be the one to complete the work in each of our children —and in each of us as parents!

Thank You, Lord, that You love our children even more than we love them. Each day of our children's lives is already determined. You know, as their Master Teacher, what they each will need (in terms of faith, character, and academics) for that future plan to succeed. We confidently depend on You for everything!

"Being confident of this, that he who began a good work in you will carry it on to completion" (Philippians 1:6).

Let Us Not Lose Heart

When Steve and I began home schooling our children, we prayed that the Lord might give us a specific verse that we could hold close to our hearts as we began this journey. He was faithful to impress this one on our hearts: "Let us not become weary in doing good, for at the proper time we will reap a harvest if we do not give up" (Galatians 6:9).

What a glorious verse that has been to claim for our family through the years! Paul begins this exhortation by telling us to "not become weary." "Christians," as Bible commentator Albert Barnes said, "Sometimes become weary. There is so much opposition to the best plans for doing good; there is so much to be done; there are so many calls on their time and their charities; and there is often so much ingratitude among those whom they endeavor to benefit, that they become disheartened...Paul exhorts them not to give over, but to persevere" (Barnes, *Notes on the Bible*, 1834).

We have needed to grow in numerous character traits over the years—creativity, patience, love, self-control, and wisdom to name a few. But more than any other character quality, Steve and I needed to persevere, to keep going no matter what, to continue year after year until we either graduated all four children (which He graciously allowed) or until God specifically spoke to our hearts to discontinue educating our children at home. Time and time again, God lovingly whispered this verse to us, causing us to persevere!

What is it that we should not lose heart doing? Paul tells us we are not to lose heart "in doing good." The Greek word for "good" here primarily means to make something "valuable or virtuous in appearance or in use." We believe that by home schooling our children we have allowed them to become more useful to God.

Although we don't know the particular plan that God has for each child, we trust Him with their future and realize that nothing from their formative years will be wasted by the God who loves our children even more than we do!

Why should we not lose heart in doing good by teaching our children at home? Because there will be a time when "we will reap."

All our prayers, efforts, tears, patience, discipline, love, planning, and teaching will bring a harvest—something tangible that we will be able to stand back and admire with amazement at what God has brought to pass.

When will this occur, this harvest we long to see? Ultimately, this will occur on the day of judgment, but it is important to understand that sometimes we won't see results from all of the above by tomorrow, or next week, or even ten years from now. But we as parents can draw comfort from the fact that there will be a time in the future when we will see the fruit of all our labors. In God's perfect timing, you will be excited and ever so grateful for what God has accomplished in your family!

But what if we don't persevere? Can we sabotage what God intends to do in our family? Could we get to some future day and weep with disappointment over the missed opportunities? We could "grow weary," Paul informs us. Thayer describes this word as meaning to dissolve, weaken, relax, or exhaust. It seems to indicate that you can relax your guard, your strength, or your resolve; you could become feeble through exhaustion; you could become tired, despondent, or fainthearted. We must pray that God will give each of us the strength and stamina not to become disheartened or lose courage when obstacles appear in our lives.

Much of this sounds relatively easy whenever we dive into a new school year, but we must be just as determined to see this project through to the end—and be just as committed to finishing the race—in January and March and May.

So, with my prayers for your success and my encouragement as a mom who has finished home schooling her children, I pass on this verse to you, so that you may constantly look to the Lord for a renewed spirit within, the courage to continue, and the desire to be obedient no matter what.

Let us not become weary in doing good, for at the proper time we will reap a harvest if we do not give up.

Put another way: "Therefore, my dear [sisters], stand firm. Let nothing move you. Always give yourselves fully to the work of the Lord, because you know that your labor in the Lord is not in vain" (1 Corinthians 15:58). May these words strengthen your hearts and minds in the days to come!

The Safe Harbor of Home

Do wintery days make you think of cups of hot chocolate, snickerdoodles, and reading with your children under a warm blanket on the couch? As Christian homeschooling families, we treasure all the moments we have together.

By deciding to obediently follow the Lord in this family adventure, we have taken the education of our children out of the hands of the public schools and placed it (where it belongs) squarely at the center of our homes.

Because the Lord is present in our hearts as born-again believers, He is able to make our homes distinctively different. We understand, better than non-Christians, that our homes need to reflect the Lord's creativity, His sense of order and beauty, His light, life, and love.

Imagine a home that welcomes you as you come through the front door. Here you are greeted with hugs and kisses and phrases like "Come on in! We've been expecting you!"

Praise music can be heard, lifting hearts and spirits to God. Other sounds, like quiet conversation, laughter, or words of encouragement, become noticeable. Homey sounds of water running, pots and pans, and dishes being put on the table make your mouth water for the dinner that is almost ready. A metronome, like a heartbeat, measures out someone's practice on the piano. A clock is ticking, occasionally chiming cheerily. Puppies chew on rawhide bones. Babies fuss, wanting to be tended to sooner rather than later. Husband and wife kiss, grateful to be together again after time spent apart.

There is a sweet scent in the air, perhaps of mountain pines or cinnamon or roses. Perhaps you can smell onions frying, freshly polished furniture, lemon soap by the sink, or old books on a shelf. You notice the fragrance of freshly washed hair or baby powder or wood smoke from the fireplace. There are fans to stir the air on muggy summer days and fur throws to wrap up in on brisk autumn ones. Shoes come off and toes wiggle in relief. Tools remain outside, briefcases are placed by the door, and travel coffee mugs are returned to the kitchen, in case they are needed tomorrow, but for now shoulders relax and the furrows in the brow smooth out. A sigh of relief releases tension in someone's chest. A glass of cold water, raspberry lemonade, or hot peppermint tea soothes the throat and revives the body.

It is the presence of details like these that make for a welcoming environment, but it is also the absence of other elements. Here there is no spiritual darkness, no fear, no disrespect, no bondage, no angry words lurking in the upper corners of the rooms, no hurtful sarcastic teasing.

Because we all still deal with a sin nature, there are occasions when we will sin against each other in our families. Anger may spill over onto other family members like hot lava or fear may cause our trust in the Lord to evaporate. But unlike families lost and helpless without the Lord, Christians know how to restore a family relationship damaged by anger or a relationship with God damaged by fear. We restore the right atmosphere by means of prayer, proper confession, and forgiveness.

Home—a haven, a safe harbor, a place where you are loved and belong, a place to restore drained energy, and to brush off the dust and irritations of a long day. It is a place of protection, both physical and spiritual. The Holy Spirit is invited to take up residence in each of our hearts and to cast His influence into every nook and cranny. I imagine ever-watchful guardian angels stationed at the four corners of our property. In the bedrooms, we have read verses like "I will lie down and sleep in peace, for You alone, O Lord, make me dwell in safety" (Psalm 4:8) and "When you lie down, you will not be afraid; when you lie down, your sleep will be sweet" (Proverbs 3:24).

Praying in the family room, we have asked the Lord to be able to "give [us] a spirit of unity...as [we] follow Christ Jesus, so that with one heart and mouth [we] may glorify the God and Father of our Lord Jesus Christ" (Romans 15:5-6).

In the schoolroom or around the dining room table we've prayed for "The fear of the LORD is the beginning of knowledge" (Proverbs 1:7) and that we might be "encouraged in heart and united in love, so that [we] may have the full riches of complete understanding... [and] may know the mystery of God, namely, Christ, in whom are hidden all the treasures of wisdom and knowledge" (Colossians 2:2-3).

Such godly homes minister to us as women, since we spend the majority of our hours in our homes. They minister to our precious children as we provide a safe and loving place for them to grow in the nurture and admonition of the Lord. Our homes grant grace and peace for our husbands to be restored after the weariness, darkness, and ungodliness of many of their places of work. And, lastly, our homes minister to those who enter, who may have never experienced a safe harbor like a Christian home. May these words from a hymn by Henry Ware, Jr., be true of us all!

Happy the home where Jesus' Name
Is sweet to every ear,
Where children early speak His fame
And parents hold Him dear.

Happy the home where prayer is heard
And praise each day does rise,
Where parents love the sacred Word
And all its wisdom prize.

Forget the Former Things

Rejoice in the gift of a new year! "Forget the former things; do not dwell on the past. See, I am doing a new thing! Now it springs up; do you not perceive it? I am making a way in the desert and streams in the wasteland" (Isaiah 43:18-19).

Perhaps some of you have had the incredible blessing of a Christian heritage passed on to you from your parents. If that is true, please take the time to thank both God and your parents, if they are still living.

For many of us, however, this verse is true: "For you know that it was not with perishable things such as silver or gold that you were redeemed from the *empty way of life handed down to you from your forefathers*, but with the precious blood of Christ" (1 Peter 1:18-19, emphasis mine).

Therefore, we just marvel at how God truly is doing a new thing in our family as well as across the nation through the homeschooling movement!

Do you perceive it in your family? It is by His grace that He is making a new way for us to live and walk in the desert of this generation, and He is causing the living water of revival to flow through the wasteland by equipping and enabling our children to be a godlier generation than our own!

God says, "I will pour out my Spirit on your offspring and my blessing on your descendants. They will spring up like grass in a meadow, like poplar trees by flowing streams." (Isaiah 44:3, 4) Pray that God will not only be gracious enough to make a new way for our families today, but also to make a new way for our children, even unto the third and fourth generation!

The enemy would be delighted if we failed to realize what God is doing, if we never caught the vision of how important our role as mothers is in His plan, or if we simply let it slip away because of tiredness or busyness.

I have long sought women to help me maintain this vision, either in person or through books. The woman who—through her writing—has most influenced me as a mother is Jean Fleming.

Here is one quote that I keep in my encouragement book, from her book *A Mother's Heart* (NavPress, 1982):

> Mothering can seem an isolated occupation unrelated to anything beyond the immediate needs of the family, but there is no more natural way for a mother to influence her world for Christ than through her own children. We will touch few lives with more intensity than the children God has placed in our homes.

The implications of this are awesome. Time devoted to our children should not be spent marking time, but as an investment in one of our greatest ministry opportunities.

Let us pray that we, as mothers, will not be weary in doing what He has given us to do—and in doing it well, by His grace. In the quietness and simplicity of daily tasks, ask God to remind you of the importance of raising godly children for Him. He will answer!

He Will Gently Lead You, Mom

"He tends his flock like a shepherd: He gathers the lambs in his arms and carries them close to his heart; he gently leads those that have young." Isaiah 40:11

Are you glad to be a mother, but sometimes weighed down by the responsibilities of being a parent? Are you exhausted? Are you overwhelmed? Does anyone hear the cries of your heart?

Oh, yes, Someone hears and is already close beside you.

The Lord is like a shepherd and He knows each one of His sheep and He especially is aware of those mother sheep, those ewes, who are nursing babies or tending young ones. You are not invisible to Him, He is looking out for you in a special way because the future of the flock rests in your hands. Without mothers to watch over, guard, protect, and love their babies, there will be no flock in the future.

"It is no accident that God has chosen to call us sheep. The behavior of sheep and human beings is similar in many ways. ...Our mass mind (or mob instincts), our fears and timidity, our stubbornness and stupidity, our perverse habits are all parallels of profound importance. Yet despite these adverse characteristics Christ has chosen us, buys us, calls us by name, makes us His own, and delights in caring for us."
W. Phillip Keller, *A Shepherd Looks at the 23rd Psalm.*

That is a humblingly accurate description of what we are, but an encouragement that He knows us well. There is no need to hide our frailties because He already knows about each one and loves us anyway. You can be completely honest with Him.

If you are a believer, then you are part of His flock and under His tender supervision. He made you, He chose you, He bought you, He calls you by your name, He makes you His very own, and He delights in caring for you.

Tell Him honestly how you feel and then let Him give you physical rest. Breathe in deeply, and with each breath remember who He is and how He loves you. Rest in His arms. Rest in His peace.

Only One Director and One Audience

Often I wonder where the balance is between retreating from the world and being caught up in a whirlwind of activities. How much stress is okay, and how much is too much? Handling a certain amount of load in our lives is a good thing.

It can be a problem, however, when life becomes overloaded. A coffee cup was designed to hold a certain amount of coffee; more than that and the cup will overflow. Four tea cups stack nicely, but the addition of a fifth cup causes the entire stack to fall over. Each of us can carry a specific amount of weight, but we cannot safely carry even five pounds more than that.

Now here's a news flash for you: as homeschooling moms, we are finite. God has lovingly designed us with limits—physical, emotional, mental, and spiritual. Physical limits are relatively easy to discern and measure, but what about your emotional limits? I can carry one person perhaps physically, but how many people can I carry emotionally? How many hundreds of questions can I answer in a day and how many decisions can I make before my life starts to topple over?

Consider this page. Do the words run from edge to edge? Is the writing solid from the top of the page to the bottom? Could you read it like that? No, it would be very hard on your eyes. Every page of type has something called margin—white space with nothing in it that enables the words to be easily read.

What does a page from your life look like? Do your days have margin? Is there breathing space, time to just be rather than do? The facts of life are these: we are not infinite, each day has no more than twenty-four hours, our energy supply is not inexhaustible, and we cannot long run on empty. Our limits are real and are not the enemy. Overloading is the enemy.

Our limits are also unique. We cannot and should not exceed these personal limits due to the expectations of other people. Consider Jesus. He did not meet every need before Him, He did not heal every sick person, or minister to everyone in Israel. He did not have an alarm clock, a cell phone, or email. He did only those things which God told Him to do which pleased and brought glory to His Heavenly Father.

In her book *Between Walden and the Whirlwind*, Jean Fleming suggests that "God is both our Director and our Audience." We have only one Director whose job it is to tell us how to live our lives. And we perform for an Audience of one, the Person we want to please the most with the way we live our lives.

What if, as an experiment, I scheduled only eighty percent of any given day (rather than one hundred percent or one hundred twenty percent)? Then there would be additional margin in my life to be available for whatever tasks God assigned. There would be time to cuddle with a little one, call a friend to encourage her, sip a cup of coffee, fix a nice dinner for my family, rest in a lawn chair and take a deep breath, read something inspirational, spend time in prayer, or just sit quietly with our little dog resting on my lap.

Try leaving margin in your day, week, or school schedule. And remember how tenderly your Director is watching over you!

The Danger of Home Cooking

Steve and I sometimes get the chance to encourage new homeschoolers just starting this adventure, and this is one analogy that we've begun sharing with them. Written by veteran homeschool dad, speaker, and author Gregg Harris, it is called "The Danger of Home Cooking."

What would you do if your neighbor, seeing you grilling hamburgers over the back fence, stepped up to you and said, "Boy, I admire you! You cook for your children every day, don't you? I could never do that!" So then he launches in with these kinds of statements:

- Only certified nutritionists should be allowed to cook.
- Home kitchen equipment can never be adequate.
- All children should eat three standardized meals per day in government cafeterias.
- Children must eat with other children to learn proper table manners.
- If everyone cooked at home, the restaurants would close and millions of people would starve to death.

Believe it or not, every one of these statements has been framed in opposition to teaching our children at home. And the amazing thing is that we don't respond to those questions, in the context of teaching, with the same kind of chuckle that we do when we hear them applied to cooking! There was a time in which the idea that people were not qualified to teach their own children at home would sound just as ridiculous!

If we don't do something about the direction of the family, and of the nation and the society as a whole, the day may come when these arguments would all be taken very seriously! We could find our kitchens under state regulation, and we could find our children required to be tested on a regular basis to make sure that they are getting all the nutritional needs that someone has decided they should have!"

Each new year, I begin with gratefulness to God that He has allowed Steve and me the privilege of home schooling—and home cooking—for our children!

As Different as Night and Day

I had been a state-licensed teacher in Colorado since before Steve and I had children, and after the Lord led us into home schooling we decided it would be best if I retained my certification in order to have the freedom to home educate our children without government control. When I needed to take six credit hours of class work in order to renew my teaching license, I enrolled in several classes at a local university, one an art class.

In the art class I made several simple projects that could be used with students of any age. Artistic expression was encouraged, so this meant that work which was unplanned, accidental, and haphazard was considered wonderfully creative. To my amazement, a sense of randomness characterized the projects done by the other teachers. But I wanted to make a pattern that made sense or expressed some message—something that was deliberate and intentional.

We dipped random objects in printer's ink and proceeded to decorate a piece of poster board. Lots of people blotted, splattered, and randomly rolled on the ink. I designed crimson paths and decorated the open spaces with a snowflake pattern made from the tips of a comb dipped in white ink. While decorating paper hats that were to say something about who we were, most people sprayed their hats with dye out of a spray bottle; I painted the ABCs on mine since I love words and teach reading! At first I didn't think too much about my choices. However, I soon came to realize that even in art I desired to make something that was as beautiful as I could create, which had an organizing structure, pattern, or symmetry. I am not saying that I was a better artist or student or anything, just that my perspective was different. One means of expression praises what is unintended, while another perspective values what is orderly. Which reflects more accurately the character and attributes of the God we serve as Christians?

The class also took a field trip to an art museum, where we were encouraged to visit galleries that displayed either modern or primitive art. The first gallery was "contemporary" with often immodest, Picasso-like paintings that kept me guessing ("Is that a rose in her teeth or is it her dinner?"). The instructor valued such art as more natural, basic, unfettered, and thus closer, somehow, to truth. But I couldn't help thinking that the primitive art reflected a worldview that omitted any notion of God and celebrated the concept of the "noble savage" and paganism.

Instead, I was drawn to the Thomas Kinkade gallery. "Traditional, pastoral, and hopeful" are words that describe these paintings—which I simply loved! The light streaming through the clouds or out of the windows of Kinkade's cottages was so magnificent, warm, and welcoming! What a distinctive world he had created, as opposed to the often dark and chaotic world designed by many other artists. Which world would I rather live in?

This class illustrated to me once again the importance of exercising discernment in every arena of life, even in something as seemingly neutral as the arts. The philosophy of the world and that which honors God must be clearly distinguished. As a Christian homeschooling parent, I always want to teach our children in a way that glorifies our Lord and acknowledges Him in every subject. That is true Christian education.

Family Celebrations

Home schooling is all about learning together as a family, not just about progressing in the academic subjects! As a Christian homeschooling family, we have always wanted to wisely use the teaching opportunities that are presented by various holidays throughout the year.

Some holidays are secular in their background (Valentine's Day), while others have a religious significance (Easter or Resurrection Day) or are patriotic in nature (the Fourth of July). So how could we use even the secular holidays as opportunities to teach about God?

I thought through each holiday with these two questions in mind. Question 1: What about this holiday is worth keeping or emphasizing in our family celebrations? Question 2: What about this holiday is not worth keeping or emphasizing?

One of my first examples of this was with Valentine's Day. Instead of making it about romantic love, I wanted to emphasize the things about Valentine's Day that highlighted God's unconditional kind of *agape* love. I collected verses like "How great is the love the Father has lavished on us, that we should be called children of God" (1 John 3:1), poured over the description of love in 1 Corinthians 13, and studied love as one of the fruits of the Holy Spirit (Galatians 5:22, 23). I looked at the commitment between a Christian husband and wife to be partners for life, which illustrated that love is a decision to do what is in the best interests of the other person, regardless of personal cost, rather than a short-lived emotion. I outlined the ways we could prepare our children for a godly marriage. I researched how love is the distinguishing characteristic of a Christian and what Scripture teaches about the heart by looking up "heart" in a concordance and reading all the verses listed. There was more about God's type of love than we could get through in the short month of February!

And with so much Scripture to use, I could avoid the secular aspects of Valentine's Day—like fleeting romantic love based on emotion and nothing else, Cupid (a mythological god) with his bows and arrows, sending "I love you" cards to those who are mere acquaintances, and encouraging relationships when children are entirely too young to consider marriage (like asking a first-grader: "Are you giving your girlfriend a card?"). Here are a few suggestions about celebrating Valentine's Day in a way that enhances your home school:

1. Study the life and the death of Valentine, a third century Roman pastor and physician, or other martyrs of the faith.

2. Study the variations of meaning for the three words translated love in the New Testament: *phileo*, brotherly love; *eros*, physical love; and *agape*, sacrificial love.

3. Memorize one verse of 1 Corinthians 13:1-13 each day in February leading up to Valentine's Day.

4. Plan an I love you family dinner with a red and white theme. The menu could include lasagna, red gelatin hearts, cheesecake with cherries or strawberries.

5. Read 1 Corinthians 13, substituting God for each use of the word love (since love is based on God's character). Then re-read, substituting your name to see how well your character matches up with God's kind of love.

6. Tell your children the story of how you and your spouse met. You can even set up a family museum with significant items representing important family events or traditions.

Blameless Before the Lord

In the checkout lane of the grocery store, the mother ahead of me announced proudly, "My daughter is going to dress up as a witch for Halloween this year!" As I tried to imagine the precious four-year old in the cart ahead of me clothed in black and wearing a pointed hat, my heart just broke. It was beyond me why anyone would want such a wonderfully innocent little child to become a walking billboard for the occult, on a day celebrating darkness. It seemed so far away from my longing to walk in the light of God's truth.

When our children were preschool and elementary age, we wanted them to know that so much of what goes on in the autumn in the name of celebrating and wearing costumes was in clear opposition to what God teaches us in the Scriptures. God tells us repeatedly that He is the God of the living. He is not the God of dead things, skeletons, witches, wizards, black magic, ugliness, scary things, blood, and gore!

So in order to teach and protect our children, we started the tradition of memorizing Deuteronomy 18:9-14 as a family during the month of October. For many years we reviewed these verses annually, each year talking in more depth about what the passage meant and how it applied to us as believers in Jesus Christ:

> When you enter the land the Lord your God is giving you, do not learn to imitate the detestable ways of the nations there. Let no one be found among you who sacrifices his son or daughter in the fire, who practices divination or sorcery, interprets omens, engages in witchcraft, or casts spells, or who is a medium or spiritist or who consults the dead. Anyone who does these things is detestable to the Lord, and because of these detestable practices the Lord your God will drive out those nations before you. You must be *blameless before the Lord* your God. The nations you will dispossess listen to those who practice sorcery or divination. But as for you, the Lord your God has not permitted you to do so (emphasis mine).

In age-appropriate terms, we defined what the words meant, what God was saying, and how we could be obedient to what He taught. Using word study tools, we found out what the words meant in the original Hebrew language. These words especially convicted me: "the Lord your God has not permitted you to do so." Not because He is some cosmic killjoy, but because He wants to protect His people from the corrupting influence of the world's system. Besides, He longs to be the one we run to with questions about our life and our futures—not a crystal ball, Magic 8 ball, Ouija board, horoscopes, or tarot cards. He wants us to desire the power of the Holy Spirit, not the powers of darkness. People who did not know Him and His loving care and concern for them would dabble in those things and become ensnared by them. But His people, the people of the light, were to be distinctively different, set apart for His purposes.

Do I love costumes? Yes! Do I love celebrating and parties? Most definitely! Do I love autumn, pumpkins, corn shocks, apples, and brightly-colored leaves? Yes! The entire fall is a prelude to the celebration of Thanksgiving for all the Lord has provided for us. I would much rather focus on these things as a family. Whenever we choose to eliminate something from our lives, I want to fill that "empty" spot with good things.

"Wouldn't a princess be better for such a little girl?" I managed to respond.

Christmas School

D r. James Dobson once wrote, "By far the most important tradition you can give your children is to instill deeply ingrained spiritual values in each child. And what better place to start than with the Christmas season." [Dobson, *Christ in Christmas* (NavPress, 1990)]. Recently I was asked by a new homeschooling mom to elaborate on a comment I had made during a talk at the annual Christian Home Educators of Colorado conference. I had mentioned the idea of Christmas School, and she wanted me to explain more about it. So I thought I would share my answer with all of you!

The idea of Christmas School, which I gleaned from one of the many home education books I've read over the years, was designed to make the Christmas holidays more Christ-centered for our family and less stressful for me. It worked particularly well during the elementary and middle school years. The idea was to take the entire month of December and change our school schedule a bit. We kept up with subjects, like math or foreign language, that seem to work best when done faithfully a little bit each day. But the bulk of our school time was spent on the projects that needed to be done for Christmas.

The children were involved in choosing a Christian card, designing and writing a Christmas letter, and addressing, licking, and stamping the envelopes. Then we could talk about how the post office gets all those letters to the homes of our friends and families. We would talk about the difference between secular and Christian Christmas cards and why our family wanted to always remind others that Jesus was the reason for the season. We also looked at the choices for Christmas stamps, preferring the traditional style to snowmen and Santa. How many stamps would we need? How much would that cost? How much per card altogether?

We would decide on presents for family that lived away from us. Many years it was something homemade or a theme basket of some sort. When did we need to mail all our presents so they would reach the cousins before Christmas? How much would each package weigh and what would the postage cost?

As the children grew, we started a tradition of exchanging names within our immediate family, instead of everyone getting a gift for everyone else. The idea was to have a modest number of presents under the tree. To help the children not become greedy before the holiday or compare the sizes and rattles of various packages, all presents remained hidden until Christmas Eve.

Together we decided what cookies to make and incorporated baking into our school schedule. Some cookies were eaten (yum!), some were frozen for later, and others were wrapped or boxed to give as gifts to friends. We made an assembly line of helpers to complete these projects, with each child doing what seemed most age-appropriate.

We played sacred, classical, or Christian carols, instead of endlessly listening to "Rudolph, the Red-Nosed Reindeer" and "Frosty the Snowman." The children were responsible for playing special requests and changing the CDs when necessary. All our Christmas music was kept in one box to make it easy to find.

We decorated the house together using artificial pine boughs, pinecones, red berries, and red velvet bows. Best of all was unwrapping and carefully placing our collections of crèches and Nativity scenes around the house. Breakable items were placed up on the mantel, while sturdy resin sets were put on the coffee table.

The Christmas tree was decorated one evening when we could all do it together, complete with finger foods and eggnog. Accompanied by Christmas music, Dad and the boys strung the lights, then everyone began decorating the tree with their favorite ornaments. Every year we have tried to give each child one special ornament, so that when the children leave home to start their own family traditions, these ornaments will be a piece of their childhood that they can bring along. The last ornament is a five-inch iron nail that we put in the very middle of the tree, so only we know it is there. Then Steve described how Christmas and Easter are related: that Jesus came as an adorable baby to grow up and be the God-Man who would deliver us from our sins.

We also have a tradition of putting a wooden cradle by the tree, empty until Christmas morning, when the baby Jesus (played by our daughter's life-size doll Elizabeth) makes His appearance. Also, one year, we collected small boxes and wrapped each in beautiful gold foil with luxurious gold ribbons and bows. Each box was given a gift tag, on which we wrote a Scripture reference that told of some gift we have because we are believers: peace, joy, forgiveness, a purpose in life, etc. On a large gold-wrapped shoebox, we explained the Gospel. All the gifts were placed under the tree in the weeks before Christmas, and when people would ask who they were for, we would explain that one gift was for those who do not yet know

Jesus Christ as their Lord and Savior and all the others were presents Christians already have!

Special books and stories are unpacked for the holidays, like *A Christmas Carol* by Charles Dickens and *The Real Twelve Days of Christmas* by Helen Haidle (Zondervan, 2000), explaining the religious symbolism of each part of the famous song. In various years, we have also celebrated Advent, along with an Advent wreath and candles, finishing up with a reading of the Christmas story from Luke.

Planning with the children helped me streamline my expectations. I found that including them in all parts of the celebration helped us arrive at the actual day more relaxed and rested than usual. Many of these ideas came out of a book called *Meeting Christ in Your Holidays* by Ann Hibbard (Wolgemuth & Hyatt, 1988):

> Christian families hold the key to joyful, exciting family celebrations. Knowing Christ infuses all of life with joy and meaning. At the heart of these special times are events that focus on Christ's life and the teaching of the Scriptures. Christmas and Easter are Christian holy days celebrating Jesus' birth, death for our sins, and glorious resurrection. Valentine's Day, Thanksgiving, and All Saints' Day or Reformation Day (as opposed to Halloween) find their source in Christian tradition and are meant to celebrate Christian themes.
>
> The significance of these holidays is all but lost in our secularized society. Baby Jesus has been usurped by a secular Santa, the risen Lord has been pushed aside by the Easter bunny, and Thanksgiving is explained as a celebration of friendship with the Indians. Christians need to reclaim the territory of our spiritual heritage. The [burden] lies on us, as Christian parents, to entrust our children with the true significance of these special occasions. Our celebrations must be distinctive, for the sake of our children and of a Christ-less world. If Christ is the center of our lives and our homes, naturally our holidays and special occasions should reflect this priority.

Christmas Simplified

Celebrating Christmas had gotten entirely out of hand. Over the years, Christmas shouted louder and louder at us. It started earlier, it got bigger, and I could no longer hear the still, small voice of Jesus through all the racket.

I recall one Christmas Steve and I celebrated when our daughter was almost one year old. We spent it with one other couple up in a cabin in the Colorado Rockies. It had a wood-burning fireplace for heat and an outhouse. There were no decorations and the meals were not fancy. Did we even exchange presents?

We talked and prayed, read Scripture, and sang Christmas carols. We sipped coffee made over the fire. The snow softened even typical outdoor sounds and there was an amazingly restorative quietness. That solitude filled my heart with gratefulness and removed many of the dents and bruises from everyday life. And that was one of our best Christmases ever.

So that year when Christmas seemed out-of-control, I talked to my husband and our now four children about what mattered the most to them about celebrating this holiday. What is the most important thing to you about Christmas? What traditions or cookies or music are meaningful to you?

Their answers permitted me to simplify. Do they want to have ten kinds of cookies and four kinds of candy? No, Steve likes chocolate fudge, that's Christmasy enough for him. The children liked best a bar cookie recipe that their Grandma Lois often made. Traditions? Camping out under the Christmas tree on Christmas Eve. Ringing the sleigh bells we had hung on the inside of the front door--that meant it was time to open presents. Being together just the six of us. Eating our traditional wake-up casserole in the morning while we watched each person open each present. It took hours! Not because there were that many presents, but because we stopped and put things together or tried things out, or changed and wore the new pajamas. This was all accompanied by appreciative oohs and ahs. There was usually a jigsaw puzzle that was kept out ready for two or three people to add some pieces as they wished.

That described our family most Christmases from then on. And we loved it! What is most important to your family? Be sure to ask them and be prepared to be surprised. It might be a simplified Christmas after all!

Teachable Moments

My sister-in-law said, "They usually sprint through the exhibits, push a couple of buttons, and they're all done in fifteen minutes. How did you keep them so entertained?" We were on a two-family outing at a museum in Arizona. The museum was practically empty, so seven cousins were let loose. All it took was less than five minutes, observing the flitting behavior of these pre-teen cousins, for the teacher inside me to rise up. So I called them back to an interesting exhibit they had overlooked.

"Look, you guys! What do you think this is?" I heard myself saying. The children wandered over to the hands-on demonstration of a *mano* and a *metate*—a pair of stones used to grind corn kernels into cornmeal. (And how did I know what the stones were called, you ask? I brilliantly read the sign just before the children came over!)

"Anybody want to try? Have you ever eaten anything made with this? How long would you have to sit here and grind flour to make enough for corn tortillas for your family's dinner?" We continued this way through the museum to emerge after almost an hour. "What interested you the most in there? What was something new that you learned today?"

Did I really keep them entertained, amused, and out of their parents' hair for an hour? Or was I using this once-in-a-lifetime visit as an opportunity to expand their horizons, teach them some Spanish vocabulary, learn about a culture different from theirs, and let them taste raw corn flour?

There are easily dozens of "teachable moments" in any given day. These are moments not scripted from a teacher's manual or part of any curriculum, but golden, real life moments that I just can't bear to let slip by. Forget *carpe diem*! Seize the moment! Opportunities like these are delightful because they teach by example and involve experiences or ideas that I permit, arrange, agree with, or want our children to experience.

Unfortunately, life is not filled only with such positive opportunities. Often there is the opportunity to teach by negative contrast, instead of by positive example. A teachable moment can come cleverly disguised—like a young guest who rudely asks what else is for dinner because he hates what we are serving; or a grandfather who launches into expletives when his football team is losing; or a television scene of two unmarried people having a physical relationship; or an announcer on a science video declaring with authority that the earth is 430 billion years old. Moments like these happen both inside and outside the haven of our homes.

How my mother's heart longs to protect our children from any and every hint of evil in the world's system! In such moments, I wish we could withdraw completely from the world. The younger our children were, the easier it was to accomplish this. But, as they grow older, the reality is that we simply cannot avoid interaction with many negative aspects of this world.

One of my favorite talks to give is on literature. I mention that, in general, there are three ways of handling literature. A parent 1) can permit a child to read everything that he gets his hands on, 2) can let a child read nothing but the Bible and a few carefully screened materials, or 3) can handle topics the way they are handled in Scripture. This third option means that as we believe our children can handle certain ideas, we will introduce them in a deliberate and thoughtful manner. Like weight training, we begin with one-pound ideas, let our children become skilled with those, before advancing to five-pound ideas and eventually working up to the really heavy ideas (we wouldn't drop a hundred-pound idea on them without preparation).

The desire is to protect our children from any harmful ideas, but it isn't practical in the long run. If they don't develop biblical discernment of their own, then we are doing them a disservice. We want to help our children recognize faulty reasoning or interpretations that don't line up with Scripture. That's why teachable moments are present everywhere. Take the woman in the grocery store who is immodestly dressed. Our children have been taught to look away and to understand that this woman is lacking something even more important than modest apparel—a healthy fear of the Lord. We should pray for God to touch her heart with the knowledge that she is created in His image and doesn't need to attract attention by the way she dresses.

Take the young house guest who is exhaustingly rude and ill-mannered for an entire eight-day visit in our home. We don't have the authority to significantly correct his behavior. Instead, we can take this opportunity to discuss godly parenting with our children. Here is an extreme example of how miserable both mother and child are when the mother is either not equipped or not willing to exercise godly parenting skills.

Can you think of other examples? How about the PBS special that assumes the validity of evolution? What material have you already covered about the theories of both evolution and creation? How do you want your children to be able to evaluate diverse theories and opinions? How would you support what you believe? How could you prayerfully, accurately, and persuasively communicate your belief to someone who thinks differently?

Daily life in this world provides many such opportunities for us to reinforce God's truths in the minds and hearts of our children. God doesn't want us to create little robots or puppets—or else we would have been born with remote controls or marionette strings. God desires us to love Him, not only with all our hearts, but also with all our minds. Therefore, we must teach our children how to discern and evaluate the ideas that come their way. Then we must give them practice in making these truths their own.

Are you unsure that you would recognize the teachable moments that come your way? Ask God to gently nudge your heart next time the opportunity arises and give you questions that will prompt your children's thinking, discernment, and godly wisdom. He delights in making you good parents for the children He has given you! Above all, please don't miss the opportunities that teachable moments provide for training ourselves and our children for effective service as a godly Christian family.

A Museum of Memories

"A museum has a selection of things worth preserving."

One year for our wedding anniversary I decided to create an arrangement in the dining room of our Indiana home. It was like a museum display of how our family started. My wedding dress, usually wrapped in plastic and tucked in the far back of our closet, was there as was our wedding album. There was a T-shirt which said, "Born at Penrose Hospital" that one of our two older children wore home from the hospital. Another tiny shirt stated "Born at Home" since our younger two were delivered by a midwife at home. Our daughter's favorite pink flannel bunny with satin binding, well-loved and well-worn, was there to bring a smile to our faces. We enjoyed it all so much that it stayed on display for over a week.

My inspiration came from a chapter in Edith Schaeffer's book *What is a Family?* She wrote, "I have always felt that [a family] is meant to be a museum of memories--collections of carefully preserved memories...Someone in the family...needs to be conscious that memories are important."

Some memories are planned, like always placing a string of sleigh bells on the inside front door to ring and gather everyone together on Christmas morning or playing Handel's *Messiah* as we open presents. Other memories just happen like all of the children sleeping beneath the tree on Christmas Eve under the multicolored lights. This then becomes a tradition, "We always sleep under the tree!"

Some memories will be sad ones while other memories will be happier. Life is filled with both. The night we slept out on the front porch, mattresses and all, until we heard a bobcat that sent us tripping over one another to get into the safety of the house. We learned the morning that our pet rabbits in the stable had become midnight snacks for the bobcat. Remember the time we ended up in Corpus Christi, TX on the gulf for an unforgettable weekend? How about the time we made a sub sandwich resembling the *Titanic* complete with dill pickle smokestacks and black olive portholes? Memories of the mountain cabin in Bailey, CO where a jigsaw puzzle was always in progress and we played the game *Balderdash* and talked late into the evening with only the fireplace embers for light. Pajama rides, birthday cakes, breakfasts in bed, building forts down by the river, camping in the backyard, swimming in the pool.

If you created a display of treasured family items, what would you include?

Wedding Anniversaries: A day to celebrate us

A wedding is a carefully planned event in the life of a husband and wife. It is filled with memories of how a couple celebrated and with whom.

A couple will celebrate only one day as their wedding but they will celebrate many more days that mark the day that wedding took place. Anniversaries measure a couple's time together and it is a special day to celebrate being us.

If you look up wedding anniversaries on the computer, you will find multiple lists of what to get a couple. There are traditional and contemporary gifts. But is that all there is to anniversaries?

This year marks Steve's and my 49th wedding anniversary. We don't really require any gifts to celebrate. Here's what we think about on this day.

Our wedding anniversary is the birthday of our family being established. We have a wooden plaque that says, "Lewis, established in 1975." When we talk with our children, it is not just a personal day for us to celebrate but it is a day for all of us to celebrate the beginning of our immediate family history.

We started as a couple but now we have grown to a family of ten--2 parents, four adult children, two additional spouses, and two precious grandchildren. So our anniversary is a celebration of what God has done in the lives of all of us. Every relationship and every anniversary has difficult times but the moments to be treasured usually outweigh the sad events. This is a good opportunity to be grateful for what God has created in this family of ours.

Our marriage is also a tangible picture to everyone of Christ's relationship with the church (see Ephesians 5:32). It is like a billboard daily announcing Christ's failthfulness and His love for the church. Anniversaries are a great time to shine up our billboards and to be sure that billboard is accurate and winsome to others.

Just as our wedding had witnesses who gathered to share in that event, an anniversary is an opportunity for those same people, and other newer friends, to celebrate again and say, "We are happy for you today as a couple. Congratulations on making it this far by God's grace. Well done."

So a wedding anniversary is a time to celebrate us, to celebrate what God has done, and to be an example of how Christ loves the church. Encourage one another on wedding anniversaries to trust completely in the Lord and to shine forth for God's glory.

Thank you, Lord, and Steve for forty-nine blessed years together. I love you!

In Peaceful Dwelling Places

The trembling squirrel, over and over again, tried to get close enough to our pool to take a drink. But we had a plastic solar cover on top, like a field of blue bubble wrap. He simply could not reach any water. After watching him for several minutes from our kitchen window, I started to think that maybe his trembling was due more to dehydration than the effort he was expending. It was one of those July afternoons when the temperature was flirting with triple digits. I filled a small bowl with cool water from the tap and set it out for him in the backyard. But, so focused on the pool water, which was filled with chemicals, he failed to notice the fresh water in the bowl.

Using this scene, the Lord brought to mind a verse from Psalms: "As the deer pants for streams of water, so my soul pants for You, O God" (Psalm 42:1). (Well, it wasn't exactly a deer I was watching, but a squirrel was a reasonably close substitute!) It made me wonder if I desire the Lord like that squirrel was longing for water. Has God set something cool and refreshing in my life that I stubbornly ignore, determined to do it on my own?

Then I considered how I was approaching the coming school year. With years of experience under my belt, my friends might think that I would know exactly how we were going to do everything this year. But, in truth, every year was different, and there were still places I struggled every single year in my preparations.

O Lord, I wondered, did You intend for home schooling to be a constant struggle? A struggle with choices, with the children's attitudes, with my attitude?

In my spirit, I sensed the Lord saying, "Come to me, all you who are weary and burdened, and I will give you rest. Take my yoke upon you and learn from me, for I am gentle and humble in heart, and you will find rest for your souls" (Matthew 11:28-29).

With eagerness, my spirit responded to His quiet voice with, "You, God, are my God, earnestly I seek you; I thirst for you, my whole being longs for you, in a dry and parched land where there is no water" (Psalm 63:1).

What would it be like, Lord, if we went through this upcoming year of home schooling sharing a sparkling, refreshing, restful outlook? Not that my year would be one long vacation, but couldn't I go about my daily routine with a renewed spirit of calmness and peace, instead of one of distraction and chaos?

> "What is the chief end of man? To glorify God and enjoy Him forever!" With great rejoicing these words have become the theme of my existence. The woven word of God has wrapped me fully round and now I wear these simple sentences everywhere. I never take them off. I sleep in the comfort of their closeness and walk with them through each day. I never tire of their pattern. I attend christenings and funeral alike in this single garment, and in this I will be buried, for it is what I want to be wearing when I meet Him face-to-face. I am clothed for all time in this apparel of praise, cloaked in the sure knowledge that I do not exist for me at all. I have been created for God. [Victoria Brooks, quoted in *Mature Daughters* by Philip G. Kayper]

This quote always encourages me. I can choose to wear the Word of God around me like a woven blanket this school year, relying on it for strength and comfort. "Show me what is important to You," I pray silently, "in each school day, Lord. Help me rest in You. Give me an unhurried spirit. Thank You for the reminder that the result of Your presence 'will be peace; its effect will be quietness and confidence forever.' (Isaiah 32:17)."

As I go through our home school year, I can rest quietly, knowing that God has called us as a family to this manner of life, that we are being obedient to that calling, and that He will provide all we need to make it through the day.

I tuck away the picture of the squirrel as a reminder to myself to choose to trust in God's provision, letting this verse soak into my soul like much-needed moisture. "The Lord your God is with you... He will take great delight in you, he will quiet you with his love, he will rejoice over you with singing" (Zephaniah 3:17).

God > Man

I have always been delighted by a poem by Carl Sandburg called "Arithmetic."

"Arithmetic is where numbers fly like pigeons in and out of your head.

Arithmetic tells you how many you lose or win if you know how many you had before you lost or won.

Arithmetic is seven eleven all good children go to heaven—or five six bundle of sticks.

Arithmetic is numbers you squeeze from your head to your hand to your pencil to your paper till you get the answer.

Arithmetic is where the answer is right and everything is nice and you can look out of the window and see the blue sky—or the answer is wrong and you have to start all over and try again and see how it comes out this time."

I love that! If your answer is right everything is wonderful, but if your answer is wrong, you have to try all over again. In this era when relativism has such a widespread influence on secular thinking, it is good to know that there are still some absolutes—answers in arithmetic are either right or wrong. Although many people assume that the study of mathematics is value-neutral, mathematical concepts can be found throughout the Bible.

Last week, we were studying about solving inequalities in algebra, a topic introduced back at the elementary level with the concepts of "greater than," "less than," and "equal to." We began to consider some biblical concepts that have either right or wrong answers. For example, Scripture teaches that God > man (Job 33:12). This would mean some other statements are true also: man ≠ God and man < God.

Yet some people do the math incorrectly and believe that man = God. That false religion is referred to as secular humanism. Remember the lie that Satan told Eve in the Garden of Eden? He said that she could be like God. Secular humanism is that lie revisited. Some philosophies teach that the world is controlled by two equal forces, the power of Evil—the dark side, if you will—and the power of Good. In the end, believers in this philosophy hope that Good will overcome or outweigh Evil. In that kind of example, the math would look like this: Satan = God. But we know from the Bible that God is the Creator and that Satan is a created being, so the math truthfully looks like this: God > Satan (1 John 4:4).

Satan forgot this. In Isaiah 14:14, we read how Satan did the math and decided that Satan = God sounded much better. This arrogance was the cause of his fall from heaven, and because many other angels also did their math incorrectly, one-third of the angels in heaven fell from grace as well.

The truth is that God > all other gods (Exodus 18:11). But, in this time of tolerance and pluralism, the math has been changed to say that God is just one of a variety of gods who may be worshipped, or that God = all gods. It is vital that we teach our children the differences in theological math like this.

Another example is in our uncerstanding of angels. We read in Psalm 8:5 that God made man a little lower than the angels; therefore, from this verse we could say that angels > man. This truth is sometimes presented incorrectly, namely, that angels = man. Take the classic holiday movie "It's a Wonderful Life." Clarence (the man) gets the opportunity to obtain his angel's wings if he assists George Bailey. It is important to clarify for our children what is "True Truth" (as Francis Schaeffer called it) and what is the creative, but incorrect, imagination of script writers. It is not biblical that humans can become angels in heaven by doing good deeds after death. Even stories that present a worthy message must be held up to the Bible in every respect.

Another truth taught in Scripture is that Jesus Christ = God the Father (John 5:18; 10:30). Many cults have done the math incorrectly and have decided either that Jesus ≠ God or Jesus < God. These cults deny the deity of Jesus Christ and maintain that Jesus was merely a prophet or a good teacher.

Lastly, here is one way to use this idea of theological math to share the gospel, using a fantastic quote from C. S. Lewis's book *Mere Christianity*. Only one of the following statements is accurate:

Jesus = liar OR

Jesus = lunatic OR

Jesus = Lord

I am trying to prevent anyone saying the really foolish thing that people often say about Him: "I'm ready to accept Jesus as a great moral teacher, but I don't accept His claim to be God." That is the one thing we must not say. A man who was merely a man and said the sort of things Jesus said would not be a great moral teacher. He would either be a lunatic—on a level with the man who says he is a poached egg—or else he would be the Devil of Hell. You must make your choice. Either this man was, and is, the Son of God: or else a madman or something worse. You can shut Him up for a fool, you can spit at Him and kill Him as a demon; or you can fall at His feet and call Him Lord and God. But let us not come with any patronizing nonsense about His being a great human teacher. He has not left that open to us. He did not intend to.

These are just a few examples of how we as parents can set a biblical foundation for math. Can you think of other ways to apply the truths of the Bible to everyday teaching?

He Will Quiet You With His Love

I know that hardly anyone in the world praises a stay-at-home mother. Even less will you find accolades for stay-at-home mothers who also choose to take on the responsibility of educating their children. Every time I find myself expecting praise and receiving censure, I am reminded by God that I am looking in the wrong place —rather like looking for roses in a compost bin!

We are not home schooling our children to please our parents or the neighbors or even our children, for that matter. We have chosen, as a couple, to home school in obedience to the Lord, since He has commanded us to raise our children in the training and instruction of the Lord (Ephesians 6:4). Steve and I were at a genuine loss about just how we could accomplish this goal if we were apart from our children for hours each day, forced to bail out many false philosophies before we could begin to instill godly thinking.

Whenever I succumb to doubt—wondering if God really cares that I have given up so much to do this, wondering what difference it will make in the end, or wondering if I am wasting my life (or being irresponsible or ruining my children, as others have sometimes indicated)—God is faithful to remind me of His sovereignty.

> Dearest daughter of mine, I am always with you! I am with you as you plan lessons. I am with you as you hug your little ones. In the darkness, I am close to you when you get up to tend a feverish one in the early morning hours. As you kneel to pray for the child with the new driver's license, I am next to you.
>
> I take great delight in you. You are giving of yourself to your children, which is the very best gift that anyone can give! It pleases Me that you will listen to My voice praising you and tune out the noise of the world.

Do you know how a nursing baby fusses when she is hungry? It only takes a minute or two, at most, to arrange your clothes to breastfeed her, but you would think that nobody ever fed this poor starving infant by the way she cries! The instant she can taste the warm milk, though, she calms down completely. God's love is soothing and calming for you, just like that milk! He wants you to be quieted and soothed in your spirit, the instant you remember His incredible love for you!

Just like in a Broadway musical, where—overcome with emotion—the actors and actresses burst into song, God sings when He thinks of you! "The Lord your God is with you, he is mighty to save. He will take great delight in you, he will quiet you with his love, he will rejoice over you with singing" (Zephaniah 3:17). When He sees the love and prayers you offer up for your children, it makes Him so happy that He breaks out in singing. How He rejoices that someone values children and is willing to give them all that they need to grow up godly and whole and healthy!

The Sin of Bickering

I have often been blessed with the opportunity to speak to home school support groups. At one such event, a question one mom raised has remained in my thoughts. Frustrated over how her children often squabbled and bickered, she asked what she should do. Should she let them work it out themselves? Do a Bible study every time they start to raise their voices? Pray that they will outgrow this childish behavior?

None of these options struck me as particularly helpful, but she was clearly at a loss. Unfortunately, as easy as it might be to lock them in a room until they work it out, my first thought was: work it out? With what skills? And doing a Bible study, as much as I cherish time to study God's Word, sounded more like punishment than instruction. As to the option of hoping they will outgrow squabbling, driving a mile or two on main roads nearly any time of the day should dispel the idea that people outgrow childish behavior on their own!

The fact is that children naturally squabble. Did you ever instruct your children in the fine art of grabbing a desired toy from the chubby hand of a sibling and yelling "Mine!" with just the right hint of indignation? Of course not! Day in and day out, I repeat patiently, "Share. You have played with that long enough. Your brother gets a turn now. Keep your hands to yourself. No pinching (biting, hitting). Be kind to your sibling. Don't call her (or him) a bozo (dumbo, fatso, four-eyes, klutz)."

People of all ages possess an innate tendency or pull toward doing what we shouldn't. The Bible refers to this pull as the sin nature. The desire to be selfish and proud and demand our rights is hardwired into each of us.

So what should a parent do about bickering within the family? My suggestion is to treat it for what it is—sin—and deal with it as God has outlined in His Word.

First, the sinfulness of the action needs to be clarified: "It is wrong to hit. It is selfish to want the bigger piece of cake. It is disrespectful to call someone, made in God's image, a name. I won't allow you to argue over a toy."

Second, the child needs to acknowledge what he or she did was wrong and repent: "What specifically did you do that was wrong? Please apologize to the person you hurt." Encourage a remorseful spirit in the wrongdoer, a sorrowful heart over the damage done within this family, and how this poor behavior broke God's heart (rather than being sorry about getting caught or sorry that your brother is overly sensitive).

Third, once an apology has been offered, determine if the relationship between the bickerers has been reestablished or if there is still more to be dealt with. The relationship is back to normal if there is an open spirit between those involved, a willingness to touch each other, and forgiveness is both offered and accepted.

The goal of instruction within the family is to put into practice all the "one anothers" found in the New Testament: love one another, forgive one another, be tenderhearted toward one another, do not lord it over one another. Now that's a curriculum guide! Why is it so crucial to deal appropriately and faithfully with the problem of squabbling (and worse) within a Christian home? Because how we learn to relate to others within the laboratory of a family is how we learn about all other relationships. The New Testament constantly uses the terms "brother" and "sister" to indicate how we are to behave within the body of Christ. And it is at home that our children learn what this looks like. To fail to encourage godly relationships at home is to handicap our children for life.

So do not get tired of praying for, intervening in, and disciplining the daily behavior of your children. The benefits are both present and future. There is the promise of harmony for your home today. There is the preparation for your children as godly parents in the next generation. And ultimately God delights to see all His children living out the truth. He is pleased to help you with the ideas, the timing, and the right words to teach your children how to act as sons and daughters of the King!

A Bouquet Lifted Up to the Lord

My heart's desire is to be a woman after God's own heart. To help me accomplish that, I really need to befriend other women and observe their walks with the Lord. Some of these ladies I have been privileged to meet in person, while others are my best friends through reading about them. So here in my writing I want to introduce you to some of these friends of mine.

One of my first friends I met through her life in words was a Dutch woman by the name of Corrie ten Boom. Her classic book called *The Hiding Place* was my introduction to her life. Many of the lessons she learned, I also learned, and carefully took to heart. There is so much to share with you from her life, but here is one incident for today.

Cliff Barrows, the longtime music and program director for the Billy Graham Evangelistic Association, shared a comment Corrie had once made during a visit to his home.

"When people come up and give me a compliment—-'Corrie, that was a good talk,' or 'Corrie, you were so brave,'-- I take each remark as if it were a flower. At the end of each day I lift up the bouquet of flowers I have gathered throughout the day and say, 'Here you are, Lord, it is all Yours.'"

Corrie's companion during the last five years of Corrie's life wrote about such a moment of offering all to the Lord.

"At the end of this tribute in Denver, after an evening full of emotional memories, looking back over a full eighty-six years, Tante Corrie was presented with a large bouquet of yellow roses. As the crowd stood to applaud her, she lifted the bouquet to the Lord and I knew she was saying to Him, 'Lord Jesus, this is Yours.'" (*The Five Silent Years of Corrie Ten Boom* by Pamela Rosewell Moore)

I remember this example when I am tempted to think I have done something in my own effort and strength. I apologize to the Lord and imagine lifting up to Him whatever little item I have in my hands. Everything we have as God's women comes from His gracious provision.

Would you join me in thanking Him today? Lift up a single yellow rosebud to Him or an entire bouquet!

Eternal Souls

Have you ever had a month that didn't exactly turn out the way you had planned? My hardest time of the year is between Thanksgiving and Christmas, so I try to plan it out in advance. We would do Christmas shopping and Christmas cards early, enjoying the process. I would prepare more home-cooked meals, in addition to some favorite cookies and breads. And we would make efficient progress in our lesson plans until Christmas break. One year, in addition to all this, I had added karate lessons with our boys and cardio-kickboxing with our daughter, and my stamina was noticeably improving. I was on a roll!

Now I am not really sure what happened. In *Winnie the Pooh*, Eeyore says, "They're funny things, Accidents. You never have them till you're having them." That's what must have occurred. I was riding the bicycle of my life serenely through fields of autumn colors—and then I was derailed, tossed over the handlebars, eating dust, totally behind.

The first derailment was being summoned for jury duty in November. The third week of that time I had to appear in federal court and ended up being selected for the jury of a civil case that took six days to settle. I had never served on a jury before, and was delighted to be serving under the senior judge in Denver, Judge Richard Matsch. Although people could be excused from serving if they could demonstrate "extreme inconvenience and severe hardship," somehow missing a week of home schooling or not being able to plan the Thanksgiving menu didn't seem severe enough...even if my dad and uncle were coming for the weekend just before Thanksgiving Day. Trying to juggle everything from afar, I began to sense that "stressed out" feeling I had been trying to avoid!

Second, my husband wanted me to attend two different conferences in Dallas with him the first week in December. Now, it seems like whenever we travel, I can do one of two things: I can get ready to leave the house or I can just leave—but I can't do both! Meals for the children, medical consent forms and insurance cards, finishing the family history books that were our gifts to relatives this year, and writing a Christmas letter all had to be accomplished.

Third, did I mention that I missed so many martial arts classes that I could hardly remember what to wear?

Deep breaths eventually cleared my mind enough to remember that my plans are just that—my plans—and God often has other things in mind. Taking time to just be with our children. Thoughtfully listen to the pain of one woman's heart, giving her— literally— her day in court. Making time for coffee with a friend, knowing that the packing can wait. Traveling with my husband because he can enjoy a business trip so much more if I share it with him. Welcoming my widowed dad and unmarried uncle for a meal around our dining room table.

It's really all about people, rather than things, isn't it? There are only a couple of things that are eternal and require our attention, time, and energy. God's Word is eternal. And the souls of people around us are also eternal. In contrast, much about this world and its system will burn up someday.

Happy New Year, Lord! Thanks for the reminder that Your thoughts are high above my thoughts, and Your ways are not my ways. Just as well. I think I'll go get a cup of coffee and see if our little pug will come sit on my lap.

Parents as Teachers

When you made the decision to become a parent-teacher, your life was forever altered. I just thought you should know. Gone are the carefree days when you only had to contend with being sure your children ate a nutritious breakfast or wore boots and coats when they ventured outside to build a snowman. Now to your already full schedule of activities, you will need to make the time to teach your children their ABCs and 123s; to say please and thank you; to know all fifty states and their capitals; to explain photosynthesis and democracy and supply and demand.

You have also taken on the responsibility to prepare them for an uncertain future. That future will involve the need to be adults who can think discerningly for themselves, communicate clearly, earn a decent living, and be godly parents to the next generation.

Being a teacher as well as a parent should not take you completely by surprise. After all, you may have already taught your son how to walk and how to throw a football. You may have already taught your daughter how to speak English and how to plant a garden. These are no small accomplishments! But now that you have become their homeschool teacher, fear and trepidation may often come flooding in. Your thoughts begin with phrases like, "But I don't know all the answers" and "How will we ever (you fill in the blank)?"

Perhaps you hated math in school (or history or having to do a group project or having to present something before your class). Now you have the wonderful opportunity to start over again and create a completely different experience for your children. Relax your shoulders. Breathe deeply. It's going to be okay.

Many homeschooling parents have a conviction from the Lord, who has put it on their hearts to teach their children. If that is true of you, then remember that what He has begun, He will also finish. Philippians 1:6 tells us that "he who began a good work in you will carry it on to completion until the day of Christ Jesus." What God finishes, He finishes well, He brings it to maturity at the right time, He fulfills His plan for each of us—parent and child.

The statistics clearly indicate that children do better academically the longer they are taught at home, that they are well-socialized in a family environment, and that they can thrive spiritually. But God is maturing the parents as well as the children. He has called your family to home school to teach you, the parent, as surely as you hope to influence your children. (Now there's a book that needs to be written—how parents benefit from home schooling!)

Parents as teachers do not need to have all the answers. It is acceptable for you to tell your children, "I don't know the answer to that question. But let's find out together!" It is arrogance that prompts us to pretend that we have all the answers. But as Christian parents we know who does have all the answers. God has incredible riches of wisdom that we have only to ask for: "If any of you lacks wisdom, he should ask God, who gives generously to all without finding fault, and it will be given to him" (James 1:5). Answers are also found in Jesus Christ "in whom are hidden all the treasures of wisdom and knowledge" (Colossians 2:3).

Although we are not expected to know everything, we should, however, be available to walk beside our children on the path of learning and continually point them in the direction of Christ, who will give our children (and us!) all the wisdom we need. In order to do this, we must maintain a home where Christ is welcomed and acknowledged in all our family does. Think of your home as a wagon wheel—from the central hub of Jesus Christ, every spoke reaching outwards represents various home endeavors: praise, worship, education, nutrition, hospitality, service, and business. When Christ is at the center of a home, everything else—including education—will prosper.

Teaching and learning will not end at high school graduation, and acquiring wisdom takes a lifetime. Parents can be the best models for a love of learning by establishing an environment that makes learning accessible. So when you made the decision to become a parent-teacher, your life was forever altered. I just thought you should know—it will be the hardest job you ever love!

Renewing Our Minds

Since Steve and I were not Christians when we did our college work in education, it never dawned on us that perhaps God had His own reasons for education, or that the Bible might have something to say about the education of our children. Becoming Christians and then starting a family caused us to re-examine what we had been taught. Needless to say, almost everything we had learned was not in line with God's thoughts and had to be jettisoned. In the words of Scripture, our minds needed to no longer be conformed to the pattern of the world's ways of thinking, but needed to be transformed and renewed (Romans 12:1-2). Today we gratefully acknowledge how completely God has changed our hearts and our minds regarding education.

One of the first things we came to understand from the Bible was that parents are charged with educating their children. Although the Bible does not specifically say which curriculum to use, it is quite clear about the topics that are most important to God. We read that we are to bring them up in the training and instruction of the Lord (Ephesians 6:4). This means that we are to raise our children to maturity specifically using two methods of training: by the use of chastening or disciplinary action, as needed, and by the use of words, whether words of encouragement, rebuke, or warning. In his *Exposition of the Bible,* John Gill says this is by "instructing them in the knowledge of divine things, setting them good examples, taking care to prevent their falling into bad company, praying with them, and... bringing them into the house of God."

Second, we learned that parents are to instruct their children about what is right. This would mean that we are 1) to teach about Jesus Christ because in Him "are hidden all the treasures of wisdom and knowledge" (Colossians 2:3), 2) teach the wisdom from above that is "pure, peaceable, gentle, reasonable, full of mercy and good fruits, unwavering and without hypocrisy" (James 3:17), and 3) we are to teach about how to take every thought captive so that we as Christians can "demolish arguments and every pretension that sets itself up against the knowledge of God" (2 Corinthians 10:5). Barnes explains this verse by saying, "The strongholds of philosophy, paganism, and sin should be demolished, and all the opinions, plans, and purposes of the world should become subject to the all-conquering Redeemer" (Barnes, *Notes on the Bible*).

It was painful to realize that the educational profession, to which we gave so much of our earlier lives, is in reality a stronghold of both worldly philosophy and man-centeredness. The first step toward demolishing such a stronghold in our family was not to permit our children to be influenced by it. The second way of combating these philosophies was to—with discernment and wisdom—destroy those opinions, reasonings, imaginations, and purposes that were in direct opposition to what we knew about God. We recognized that this would be a long process of allowing God to transform our minds, and we asked Him to do this through everything we learned as a family.

Third, we as parents are not to teach what is wrong. This sounds rather obvious, I know, but think about that for a minute. There is a kind of wisdom, not from God, that is "earthly, natural, and demonic" (James 3:15). Which kind of wisdom are you providing for your children: the wisdom that is from the world or the wisdom that is from above?

As Christians, we are to see to it "that no one takes [our children] captive through hollow and deceptive philosophy, which depends on human tradition and the basic principles of this world rather than on Christ" (Colossians 2:8). There is the direct command to "not conform any longer to the pattern of this world" (Romans 12:2). We want to avoid, for us and for our children, the possibility that we could be "always learning but never able to acknowledge the truth" (2 Timothy 3:7). Knowledge without the correct foundation of faith and character causes a person to be literally puffed up or inflated with pride (1 Corinthians 8:1). But knowledge tempered with God's kind of love edifies us, building up our faith like a house constructed on a firm foundation.

Would you and your spouse consider taking the time soon to look up each of these verses and consider what God is saying to you regarding the education of your children? In what educational setting can you best bring your children up in the training and instruction of the Lord?

The Character Quality of Obedience

The character quality of obedience was one that continually needed practice in our house. (I'm sure that's not the case for you and your family, right?) And whenever we were working on it, God was faithful to bring my attention to scenes outside of the house that emphasized the why behind this quality.

Scene 1: a toddler single-mindedly heads for the front door of the library. "Tommy! Come here," the mother calls. No response. "Okay, I'm going to count to three. One...two...Tommy, are you listening to Mommy? Three! Okay, Tommy, now Mommy's really mad!" (Afterwards, in the car, we talk about how parents are the God-given authority over their children and need to train them to obey immediately, instead of when Mommy gets to number three.)

Scene 2: a pair of children misbehaving in the grocery store. "Jessica, sit down in the cart. Michael, stop running in the aisle! Look where you're going. Jessica, you are going to fall out and crack your head. Get back here, Michael, I mean it, right now!" (This one made me glad for all the times we talked about public behavior before we left the house...and even the times I left my cart half-full and walked out with a misbehaving child, determined that character training trumped grocery shopping.)

Scene 3: teenagers in a class. "Now we're going to work on the four-step combination we learned last week," the karate instructor says. "Actually, last week we did the nine-step combo," one student pipes up. "Well, today we're working on the four-step one." "But not everyone's learned that yet," he persists. Frustrated, the teacher explodes, "We're doing it my way today!" (Glancing at my boys' red faces, I am glad that they have learned how to respectfully correct or make an appeal to someone in authority...and definitely not to do it in public.)

Scene 4: adult drivers in a busy intersection. With a new driver at the wheel, I watched as four or five cars slipped through the tail end of a yellow light, some of them after it had already turned red. Although watching to make sure we didn't get involved in an accident, I was relieved to see my son stop at the next yellow we came to, instead of following the example of those other impatient drivers who thought the laws about traffic lights didn't really apply to them.

These scenes, and many others like them, remind me that obedience isn't something you learn once, but a lesson that continues all life long. A character quality is a habit you develop through repeated practice. And Christian character is especially important, because we are reflecting the traits of Jesus Christ in our lives to a lost world (Romans 8:29).

Our working definition of obedience has always been "to promptly, cheerfully, and completely carry out the directions of those in authority over me." This included learning the importance of boundaries and yielding the right to have the final decision.

So how are you and your family doing at learning and demonstrating the quality of obedience? Since it's often hard to judge, here are some questions to help you evaluate your family's current state of obedience.

1. Do your children ask for reasons when their requests are turned down? Obedience means accepting "no" as the final answer, without questioning, whining, or discussing it.

2. Do your children stop what they are doing immediately when given instructions? Obedience means acting on commands immediately, without delays or objections.

3. Do your children have a pleasant facial expression when they are told to do something? Obedience means cheerfully responding to requests, without frowning, groaning, complaining, or rolling eyes.

4. Do your children ever give reasons why they cannot do a job? Obedience means finding ways to overcome obstacles, rather than using negative thinking as an excuse to get out of it.

5. Do your children have to be reminded to do little tasks? Obedience means following through on little commands as well as big ones, without justifying inattention or making excuses.

6. Do your children ever have to redo a job they did wrong or sloppily the first time? Obedience means following all orders thoroughly the first time, without assuming, guessing, forgetting, or self-will.

7. Do your children ever complain that a job is stupid? Obedience means doing jobs even without knowing the reasons behind them, without mocking, whining, or questioning.

8. Do your children ever go ask one parent after receiving a "no" from the other? Obedience means not pitting one authority against another, with no scheming or withholding important facts.

9. Do you obey whatever God tells you to do? Obedience is based on what God says is right and true, while also taking personal responsibility for your actions.

Adapted from *http://CharacterJournal.com/category/obedience/*

If, after going through this list, you like your progress as a family, then take some time to specifically praise your children and let them know you are proud of the way they are developing godly character. If there are areas where you and your children struggle, prayerfully decided how you can focus on this character quality as a family, making it a priority to develop your obedience muscles so that you can be better servants of Christ and ambassadors for God.

Derailment or Opportunity?

Ever feel that your home school schedule has been derailed by the other events in your life? You finally settle into a routine, humming along, then it happens—some major life event intervenes, turning your carefully organized schedule upside down. "We interrupt this home school year to bring you ..." Pick one of the following: a major family move, an illness, a job transfer or change, a surgery and recovery time, a new baby, etc.

We have learned as a family that home schooling does not occur in a vacuum. The rest of life is not put on hold while we "do" school. Yet it is easy to assume that when the academics seem to be sidelined for a time, our home school is a failure. If academics were the only thing we were responsible for as homeschooling families, then I guess a failure to accomplish that would be a derailment. But God deals with us as a total package, both individually and as family units. His ultimate goal is for each of us to be conformed to the image of His son, the Lord Jesus Christ (Romans 8:29). And He will use whatever it takes to accomplish that in our lives. Academics is a part of the total package, but only a part. There is much we need to learn about faith and character, God and His world, and relationships with others.

After enduring many a derailment in the twenty years of our home schooling adventure, our current situation involves a critically ill mother-in-law. About five years ago, Steve's mother, Lois, moved to live about two blocks away from us. Two years later she was diagnosed with a genetic disorder that causes lung and liver damage. Vibrant and energetic when she arrived, she has had a difficult last few months, declining steadily throughout the year. One nursing home stay, four hospitalizations, two emergency room visits, and a year of weekly infusions have changed our homeschool schedule dramatically. This past week, with her liver in almost complete failure, and an unexplained severe weakness, she was re-hospitalized and then moved to a nursing home, probably not to return to her home again.

No, we have not completed as many pages of Peter's American Government text as I had planned. But it is God Himself who has arranged our curriculum this fall to include classes in Advanced

Prayer, Liver and Lung Anatomy 101, Independent Studies, How to Clean Two Houses (when keeping just one is challenge enough for me!), Compassion, Caring for the Elderly, Flexibility in Time Management, and Honoring Parents/Grandparents 201.

So thank You, God, for the curriculum You have lovingly designed for us as a family this year. We have learned and stretched and prayed more than ever before. We have come to trust You in an even deeper sense than a year ago. There have been many frustrating interruptions in my plans and expectations, but God's plans have hummed along right on schedule! This is individualized learning at its very best.

Preventing Burnout

Ever feel as a homeschooling mom that you are trying to juggle too many balls, constantly losing your grip on one or another? Are you feeling overcommitted, overwhelmed, overtired, or overburdened? If you are already feeling tired and weary, how are you going to add holiday responsibilities to a full schedule, or deal with life stresses like pregnancy, illness, or lost jobs?

Burnout occurs when a mom becomes "overloaded for an extended period of time." According to Steve and Mary Farrar in *Overcoming Overload* (Multnomah, 2003), there are at least three circumstances that seem to push us into overload: the pace of life, the pressures of life, and the pain of life.

The pace of life is just the sheer volume of things we have to handle on any given day. When I was a young mother, I could go to the grocery store for toothpaste and choose between two basic kinds: Colgate and Crest. Nowadays there is a whole aisle just for toothpaste! Colgate offers 56 types of toothpaste: for preventing plaque and gingivitis, for fresh breath, for cavity protection, for tartar control, for whitening, for children, and for sensitive teeth. Crest comes in a gel, a liquid gel, or a paste, or in various flavors like cinnamon or mint. (I feel a stress headache coming on!)

It is also easy to reach our point of overload due to the pressures of life. These pressures often result from the conscious choices we have made. But having made what we thought were good choices, we now realize that we have no more elbow room or breathing space left in our lives. One solution might to be to simply avoid any and all kinds of stress. In reality, however, that will probably never happen. If it did, we would probably complain that life was routine, boring, and predictable!

Life can also involve pain from circumstances that are often out of our control: the loss of a job or a loved one, a major move, financial difficulties, sickness, problems in pregnancy, or infertility. The solution to avoiding burnout (makes me think of a burnt raisin smoking in the bottom of the toaster!) seems to be in learning the difference between a basic, everyday load and an unhealthy overload. Overloading happens when a person exceeds her limits. Think of it like the capacity signs of a public theater—for every space, no matter the size, there is a limit to how many people can safely fit there. Could you carry a twenty-pound preschooler? Probably. Could you carry five preschoolers? Probably not. How much is too much for you, and when is enough truly enough?

It is interesting how we can distinguish between real-world burdens that are too heavy (you wouldn't unload a fridge from a moving van by yourself, right?), but emotional overload is not so easy to spot. We tend to pick up, without much thought, too much emotional baggage.

There's no shame in admitting your limits. In fact, overloading yourself can fall into the category of trying to be like God—infinitely wise, all powerful, and never needing sleep. God is well aware of our finiteness. In Psalm 103:14 He reminds us that "we are dust." Not exactly a flattering description of a generation of women who have been led to believe that we can do it all!

The truth is that we cannot do it all. We each have our own unique and individual limits. We only have twenty-four hours in each day, we each have only so much energy, and we each require a certain amount of sleep per night to keep us sane, let alone refreshed! We compare our own limits with other women at our own peril.

To avoid burnout, here are four guidelines to consider. First, set healthy boundaries for yourself—learn to distinguish between what is good and what is best. What are the good things that fill your day? Do these good things get in the way of any best things? Practice saying "no"—in front of the mirror, if you need to! When someone asks you to consider any new responsibility, realize that something you are currently doing will have to be bumped to make room for the new activity. Is that truly how you want to use your time? Instead of giving an instant answer, ask for time to pray about a new responsibility and consult your husband. Many times Steve has wisely told me to decline an offer because he is well aware of how I am handling (or not handling!) what I currently have on my plate.

The next guideline is to leave extra space in your life and in your day. Some authors have referred to that as "margin." What if this article filled the entire page—would it still be easy to read? Not really. So does your life have space around it? Do you have time at the end of the day, money at the end of the month, and energy by late afternoon? What if you scheduled only 80% of your life instead of scheduling 120% of it? What if you allowed time to listen to God's voice or kept some energy, joy, money, or hugs, in reserve for when they are most needed?

Third, make every effort to get enough rest. Be sure you get enough sleep at night (even if that means dirty dishes in the sink or unanswered emails). If you have children that nap, lay down for a rest too, instead of cleaning the house. What are activities that relax both you and your children? Perhaps taking a walk, watching cloud formations lying on your backs in the grass, taking a couple of deep breaths, blowing soap bubbles, playing praise music throughout your home, or snuggling together on the sofa with a good book will create extra elbow room for you.

Fourth, determine what are family activities you and your husband most value and plan your week so that those things take priority. One year, swamped by the expectation that Christmas would only be Christmas if I baked fifteen different kinds of cookies, I asked my husband what mattered most to him. He said Christmas would be perfect if I would just make him some fudge. That's it? Just fudge? I could do that! And the time I would have used to make fifteen dozen cookies was suddenly mine again, along with more joy and less stress!

If you and your family took time to sip hot cocoa and enjoy your Christmas tree lights, but you never got around to decorating the mantel, would the holiday be ruined? Probably not. The years we have enjoyed the holidays the most were the ones where we deliberately throttled back on the expectations and had time to just be together. So here's to more breathing room, more elbow room, more margin, and more joy in our lives!

This Lamb Loves You, Lord

"Shout joyfully to the LORD, all the earth. Serve the LORD with gladness; come before Him with joyful singing. Know that the LORD Himself is God; it is He who has made us, and not we ourselves; we are His people and the sheep of His pasture. Enter His gates with thanksgiving and His courts with praise. Give thanks to Him, bless His name. For the LORD is good; His lovingkindness is everlasting and His faithfulness to all generations." Psalm 100

Dear Lord,

Walking out our front door, we are met by a blaze of sun lighting up the trees in the park across the street. All the earth, this psalm says, shouts with joy to the Lord. It is so glorious an autumn day that I believe all the shimmering gold and scarlet trees are indeed shouting joyfully! And I want to join in praising You.

One way I can praise You is to take this psalm and pray it back to You. This can be a devotional practice with any portion of Scripture. So here goes...

As I shout joyfully, I will decide to serve You this day with gladness in my heart and a smile on my face. I will sing songs of praise about how amazing You truly are.

The psalm reminds me that you are the Creator. Here is a truth about the correct order of the world--You made me and not the other way around. You made me and each member of our dear family. I thank You, Lord, for making my husband and bringing us together in Your time. Thank you for the children You also made and have blessed us with.

We are Your people and it is such a joy to belong to You. This lamb loves You and is ever so glad to be a part of Your flock, Lord. You are our Shepherd who takes excellent care of us.

We bless Your name for You are good in every single way. How amazing to think that Your lovingkindness stretches forever. You have been faithful to all the generations that love, serve, and follow You. I especially see it in our lives.

With love from one of Your special lambs.

Is Being a Mother Valuable?

God has used many amazing, precious women to be my mentors in Christian womanhood through the years. I am grateful for the lessons I have earned from each woman. But my all time favorite book on motherhood is Jean Fleming's book *A Mother's Heart: A Look at Values, Vision, and Character for the Christian Mother.*

Values, vision, and character -- three foundational elements I needed to become a Christian mother. I had absolutely none of those.

Growing up in a non-Christian home gave me no reason to think a Christ-honoring home was valuable. I had no vision for the job and no clue what such a home might even look like. I began with little character, but Christian motherhood comes with its very own on-the-job training program for character development.

Is being a mother valuable?

Jean shared, "If you are a mother, you have a calling from God. God entrusts into your care a life, a future, a piece of what the world will become."

Pastors refer to being called by God into the ministry. Missionaries usually can remember a time when they felt led or called by God to minister in whatever capacity He shows them. If you have a child growing inside you or snuggled in the hollow of your arm; or if you anticipate holding an adopted son or daughter in your arms in the near future, guess what? You too have been called into a ministry by God!

You have been called to be a steward as well. A steward is a person who manages the affairs of another, rather like Joseph was to Potiphar in the book of Genesis. A steward doesn't own what he or she manages, but is responsible to faithfully care for everything given into his or her capable hands.

A baby is given by God into the responsible hands of parents to raise that child to maturity. The parents do not own any child, nor does the government own our children. God owns the children as they all come from Him. Our job as parents is to --as the saying goes -- give them roots and give them wings for God's glory.

Jean ends her first chapter with these words, "It isn't that mothers can't do many other things, but if they refuse to accept their calling as mother some child ends up shortchanged. And the empty space that mother leaves echoes for generations."

Is being a mother valuable? Most definitely yes. Do you feel called?

Mothering is Your Ministry

"You are as much serving God in looking after your own children, and training them up in God's fear, and minding the house, and making your household a church for God, as you would be if you had been called to lead an army to battle for the Lord of hosts."

Charles Spurgeon

We were finishing up our Bible study on the book of Matthew. Just two more verses to discuss. "Then Jesus came to them and said, "All authority in heaven and on earth has been given to me. Therefore go and make disciples of all nations, baptizing them in the name of the Father and of the Son and of the Holy Spirit" (Matthew 28:18-19). Reading these verses caused my precious friend to wilt emotionally. "I am not doing anything about this command from Jesus! I am just a stay-at-home mom with no important ministry. Every time I read these verses, I feel like such a failure."

These verses are such a stirring call to make disciples as we go through our lives. But I also understood why my friend might feel so dismayed. The world around us attaches little value to the profession of motherhood.

"Hello, what do you do?" I have been asked.

"I am a mother to our four children," I said, as a former public school teacher turned stay-at-home mother."

"Oh." The answer dropped like a rock to the floor. Silence followed. Then the subject was changed.

But here is the truth about motherhood from God's perspective: if you have children, you automatically have been assigned an incredibly important ministry. Children make up families. Families are the building blocks God uses to build a society. To support a society, the families need to be strong and healthy. The children God has given us need safe, welcoming, loving, and godly homes in which to grow.

Our children need to grow up like our Lord did. "And Jesus grew in wisdom [intellectually] and stature [physically], and in favor with God [spiritually] and man [socially]" (Luke 2:52).

We have heard and, unfortunately, may have believed a monstrous lie, "Being a mother is not important and it definitely is not a ministry." We need to deliberately and diligently replace that lie with the truth that each mother has a ministry to her children that no one else can fulfill. By God's design, your children need you and you need your children.

Our families are our primary ministry and our children do not get in the way of "real" ministry.

If you have children, as you go about the business of life, consciously decide to make your children disciples, followers of the Lord Jesus Christ. Make Christ known to them. Acknowledge Him in your home. Pray for them to have a personal relationship with the Lord as soon as He calls them, and encourage them to be baptized in order to identify with Christ. Teach them all that He taught us through the Word and Himself. And remind your children that Jesus is with them always, even until the end of this age.

This is your ministry. This is your challenge, career, and profession. May God bless the work of your hands.

"Children are not a distraction from more important work. They are the most important work." C.S. Lewis

God's Opinion That the World Should Go On

Why did God entrust precious babies into our care? Was it so the baby would be tenderly loved and grow to maturity? Or was it so the parents would have the opportunity to practice unselfish love and mature themselves? Perhaps God's perfect plan involves equal amounts of both.

"A baby is God's opinion that the world should go on," wrote poet Carl Sandburg. Each new baby is evidence that God affirms life. The Lord has permitted Steve and me to welcome into our home four such indicators of His desire that the world continue. For many years now, we have watched these children grow in the wisdom and knowledge of Jesus Christ. And while we were so intent on raising them up, God was also intent on maturing the two of us.

One day I was buckling Timothy into his car seat in our gold Volkswagen. When I finished, I closed the door and walked around to the driver's seat. Timothy burst into tears, wailing like I was deserting him for good. Annoyed, I got in and shut the door. Why would he cry like that? When had I ever left him to fend for himself in all his eighteen months of life?

Gently, I sensed God speaking to my heart, "Vicki, I have seen you cry like that."

Even more annoyed, I thought back, "When have I ever cried like that, Lord?"

"Every time you panic and think I won't take care of you. Like when Steve resigned from his job and you jumped to the conclusion that now you would all probably die of starvation. Did I let you starve then?"

"Or what about after a few weeks of fruitless house-hunting, when you announced that I probably wanted your family to live in a sleazy, crime-ridden neighborhood. Aren't you living in the perfect house, white with yellow shutters, near Steve's work, and for exactly the amount of money you had in hand?"

Chagrined, I leaned my head against the steering wheel. "I'm deeply sorry, Lord. Please help my faith in You to grow."

Zephaniah 3:17 says, "The Lord your God is with you, he is mighty to save. He will take great delight in you, he will quiet you with his love, he will rejoice over you with singing." Isn't that a great verse for a maturing mom to read and re-read? God is always with you as you go through your day—you are never all alone with your children. He takes great delight in how you care for, love, nurture, and discipline the children He gave you. When you are feeling scattered, nervous, weary, or frantic, remember that He will soothe and quiet you with His unfailing love—you have only to remember that your efforts to be a godly mother are both seen and appreciated by Him. Rejoicing at how far you have come as a mother, He breaks into songs of thanksgiving for you.

As parents, we have the responsibility to raise our children to maturity for the Lord. But I hope I never forget that God is also in the business of raising up Christian parents to maturity for Him as well.

Names for Our Children

If you have done much reading in the Old Testament you know how names are important to the Jewish people. The meanings of the names that babies receive often indicate, and hopefully encourage, good characteristics and future blessings.

When it comes time to consider naming your child or children I would like to make several suggestions.

Pray about the right name for your child. God knows every day of this child's life and every aspect of his or her character so ask Him directly. What would You have us name this baby, Lord?

God put it on our hearts to give our children names they could grow up into. Nothing silly or cute but something dignified. Imagine your child at his first job interview, shaking hands with the boss, and introducing himself.

You could use the names of historical figures in the Bible. Each of our sons ended up with one Old Testament name and one New Testament name. So we had Jonathan Andrew, Timothy Daniel, and Peter Joseph.

Our daughter, who is the oldest, was named Amanda Christine which we defined as "Beloved Follower of Christ." Amanda is a Latin form of "Beloved" and Christine is like Christian, "one who follows Christ."

You could use the given or middle names or surnames of family members you would like to honor. My dad was given the Bible name of Mahlon (his family pronounced it MAY-lon) which is Hebrew for "sick, pining." It sounded like a name that should have been rejected based on its biblical meaning. But he was actually named after his maternal grandfather. The grandfather had practically banished his daughter over her choice of husband. Naming their son after him was an attempt to make peace.

We prayed that God would show us a Bible verse or verses that went along with each name. We researched to learn possible meanings and chose a verse that reflected that meaning. We also asked Him for a meaning and verses that went with my husband's and my names and our surname.

Over the years, we had several editions of these name verses hanging over the sofa in our family room. I learned calligraphy by hand for the first set. Each of us had both our first and our middle names with verses on 8" x 10" parchment-colored paper that were individually framed. There was another edition made when script fonts came into style. These were so much easier to make than the hand-calligraphed copies.

The last style we had was one frame with nine openings in it. Our information went into six of the openings, our surname went into a seventh, and two of the openings had decorations rather than names in them.

When the children moved out or we moved, the frames were turned over to the individual to keep and the wall arrangement in the family room was dismantled.

Reading the names, meanings, and verses over the years has given us ample time to reflect on the names, to be encouraged, to praise God for how He has grown us all up in Him, and to stand a little straighter and taller in trying to live up to the meaning of the names. Perhaps you might like to make something similar for your family. Because He first loved us and each of our names matters to Him.

Gentle Lullabies for Babies

"When the bough breaks, the cradle will fall, and down will come baby, cradle and all."

Humming this to our first child, I quickly realized that I didn't want to sing to her about babies falling out of dangerous trees and getting hurt!

So I tried out the second lullaby in my repertoire, "Hush, Little Baby." There was no falling out of trees in this nursery rhyme. Instead, lots of things go wrong: a mockingbird won't sing, a diamond ring turns brass, a mirror gets broken, a billy goat refuses to pull a wagon, a cart driven by a bull flips over, a new dog won't bark, a horse and cart fall down, but Papa will fix everything and you will still be the sweetest baby in town!

That wouldn't work either! I needed some new material! I wanted to sing to our baby about how Jesus loved her, how she was special to her heavenly Father and to us, and how she was safe in His arms.

Michael Card's lyrics came to the rescue! "Sleep sound in Jesus, my baby, my dear, angels are watching, they keep you so near; know for His sake you'll be safe for the night, sleep sound in Jesus, I'll turn out the light." That's exactly what I wanted to sing and, often, that was exactly what my heart needed to hear.

One of the lullabies is entitled "Barocha" (pronounced bah-RUKE-ah) which is the Hebrew word for "blessing." Using the words from Numbers 6:24-26, the blessing that Aaron used so long ago, soothes our modern-day hearts.

These are off the Michael Card CD "Sleep Sound in Jesus." I have often used this as a baby gift for friends, but it would also be a great CD for anyone looking for peace as they drift off to sleep. "In peace I will both lie down and sleep, for You alone, O LORD, make me to dwell in safety." Psalm 4:8

Greater Joys of Little Girls and Boys

I want to talk about Christian parenting, and I especially want to share God's words from the Bible with you. But I also want to introduce you to the words of other authors who give us fresh insight into daily living and whose words uphold the values God sets before us.

The world around us often blares, as if through a megaphone, that young children--especially babies--are an inconvenience and a dreadful nuisance. I happen to love Edgar A. Guest's poem "Tied Down" in response to that kind of statement. Try reading it aloud to family or friends. Enjoy!

'They tie you down,' a woman said,
Whose cheeks should have been flaming red
With shame to speak of children so.
'When babies come you cannot go
In search of pleasure with your friends,
And all your happy wandering ends.
The things you like you cannot do,
For babies make a slave of you.'

I looked at her and said: "Tis true
That children make a slave of you,
And tie you down with many a knot,
But have you never thought to what
It is of happiness and pride
That little babies have you tied?
Do you not miss the greater joys
That come with little girls and boys?

'They tie you down to laughter rare,
To hours of smiles and hours of care,
To nights of watching and to fears;
Sometimes they tie you down to tears
And then repay you with a smile,
And make your trouble all worth while.
They tie you fast to chubby feet,
And cheeks of pink and kisses sweet.

'They fasten you with cords of love
To God divine, who reigns above.
They tie you, whereso'er you roam,
Unto the little place called home;
And over sea or railroad track
They tug at you to bring you back.
The happiest people in the town
Are those the babies have tied down.

'Oh, go your selfish way and free,
But hampered I would rather be,
Yes, rather than a kingly crown
I would be, what you term, tied down;
Tied down to dancing eyes and charms,
Held fast by chubby, dimpled arms,
The fettered slave of girl and boy,
And win from them earth's finest joy.'

Child Evangelism Fellowship

I first heard of Child Evangelism Fellowship when our daughter was a toddler. We knew we wanted to begin teaching her about the things of God. Only I had no idea how.

The problem was that I had become a born-again believer three or four years earlier and I had neither the knowledge nor the vocabulary to share anything spiritual with her. I learned about CEF so that I could teach Amanda.

Child Evangelism Fellowship "is a Bible-centered organization composed of born-again believers whose purpose is to evangelize boys and girls with the Gospel of the Lord Jesus Christ and to establish (disciple) them in the Word of God and in a local church for Christian living."

The ministry was founded in 1937 by Jesse Irwin Overholzer. At the age of twelve, he was aware of his sin and his need for forgiveness. When he went to his mother, she told him he was too young to understand the Gospel. Jesse would not hear the Gospel until he was in college.

As a pastor, Jesse read a comment from one of C.H. Spurgeon's sermons which said, "A child of five, if properly instructed can as truly believe and be regenerated as an adult." This led Jesse to begin a ministry designed to reach out to children from a young age with the good news about Jesus Christ.

We found this to be true with all four of our children. Amanda gave her life to Jesus the Easter when she was four years old. Our sons, similarly, professed Christ as their Savior at the ages of four to six.

Some of the products published by CEF that we continued to use over the years were the Wordless Book, the CEF Bible lessons (which clearly present the gospel on a child's level), and *The Children's Ministry Resource Bible*. This is designed to be used by teachers and parents with children ages 5-12.

He wants all the little children to come to Him. If you are a parent, a grandparent, or you want to minister to children, find out what this ministry has to offer. You will be glad you did.

The Wordless Book

In a sermon preached in 1911, Charles H. Spurgeon began like this,

> "I daresay most of you have heard of a little book which an old divine [a minister of the gospel] used constantly to study, and when his friends wondered what there was in the book, he told them that he hoped they would all know and understand it, but that there was not single word in it. When they looked at it, they found that it consisted of only three leaves; the first was black, the second was red, and the third was pure white. The old minister used to gaze upon the black leaf to remind himself of his sinful state by nature, upon the red leaf to call to his remembrance the precious blood of Christ, and upon the white leaf to picture to him the perfect righteousness which God has given to believers through the atoning sacrifice of Jesus Christ his Son."

Later, a gold page was added to depict the love of God and the glories of heaven. D.L. Moody used a booklet of four colors to speak to a crowd of 12,000 about their need for Christ. Fanny Crosby kept a wordless book in her purse and she shared about her beloved Savior at any opportunity. In 1895, Amy Carmichael took the little book to India. She had a satin flag made with the four colors and raised that flag over her oxen cart. Going from small town to small town, the flag was a good conversation starter.

Child Evangelism Fellowship (CEF) began using it in the 1920s after the founder's wife, Ruth Overholtzer picked up one in the bookstore of the Moody Church in Chicago after the pastor at that time, Dr. Harry A. Ironside, had found it in London. CEF added one more page, a green one, to represent Christian growth.

Quite a long trip for such a small book! CEF says, "Although colors have been added over the years, the story it tells has never changed. Each time someone shares the wordless book, those listening learn about Heaven and God's love for them, the darkness of sin, the blood of Christ, a clean heart, and how to grow in Christ."

It is a great tool to use with anyone but especially with children. Children understand it easily and can share the story with other children.

The Wordless Book is available from CEF Press and comes in three sizes, a little one that is 2" x 3" for small hands, a medium-sized one that is 3.5" x 3", and a large or classroom-size one that is

8.5" x 11". It comes with instructions on how to share it and appropriate Scripture verses to use.

He is patient with you, not wanting anyone to perish, but everyone to come to repentance (2 Peter 3:9). That means you and your children.

Be Careful Little Eyes

Have you ever eaten a bit of meat only to discover that hidden away in that bite is a nasty piece of gristle? What do you do with that gristle? Do you roll it around in your mouth, examining how big it really is and whether you could swallow it without choking? Or do you get rid of it as quickly and as discreetly as possible, hoping not to gag openly at the dinner table, and then proceed more cautiously with the remainder of your meal, concerned that other unidentified objects may be lurking?

Even when offered an entire buffet, we should approach the table with common sense and much discernment. Not all the items offered may be good. The food could be poorly prepared, not maintained at the correct temperature, or the ingredients might be spoiled. Some of the items may be all right for one person to consume, like something made with chocolate, peanuts, or wheat flour, yet might cause a severe allergic reaction in another diner.

Oh, be careful, little eyes, what you see...

Our mouths are not the only way we ingest things from the world. Much information, moral or immoral, comes in through our eyes. For example, how do we respond when we see a woman or girl who is dressed immodestly, demonstrating that she has no fear of God in her heart? Do we use common sense and discernment when selecting what to set before our eyes in the form of movies, television shows, artwork, and books? Do we act as promptly to remove an offending sight from our field of vision as we would if we discovered an unwanted fish bone in our dinner?

"I will set before my eyes no vile thing," instructs Psalm 101:3. Vile or worthless means being good for nothing or wicked. Studying God's Word diligently will give us the practical knowledge we need to be able to parent in a godly way and discern what is good for something and what is good for nothing. Continually praying and asking for God's wisdom and discernment goes hand-in-hand with studying the Scriptures.

Oh, be careful, little ears, what you hear...

Every day the world's smorgasbord offers a wide array of auditory input. Some of the items on that menu are soothing and commendable, like a Bach sonata or a child's giggle. Others are detrimental, like the harsh sound of angry words between a parent and a child or the sting of blasphemous words spoken against our Lord Jesus. As godly parents, we need to understand that we should always be on the alert for those things which might endanger our family's physical and spiritual well-being.

How quickly do we parents identify a piece of philosophical gristle in something we have just read and taken into our minds? How quickly do our children identify the presence of unbiblical ideas in their daily lives? The solution is to listen to the truth of God's Word. "Whether you turn to the right or to the left, your ears will hear a voice behind you, saying, 'This is the way; walk in it'" (Isaiah 30:21).

Oh, be careful, little hands, what you do…

A hand can lovingly rumple a child's hair, wipe away a solitary tear spilling down a cheek, or bring Mama a fistful of dandelions. That same hand could, however, grab a child by the wrist in anger or slap a child's face. These kinds of things should not occur, by the grace of God, in any Christian home. "The wise woman builds her house, but with her own hands the foolish one tears hers down" (Proverbs 14:1).

Oh, be careful, little feet, where you go…

Where do we walk? Where do we take our children? How do we live out our lives, under the watchful eyes of our children? "This is the way, walk in it." Do we go together as a family to a church where God's Word is taught and honored? Do we avoid places that might be harmful to our Christian walk, testimony, or character-building? Are we actively doing things that would make God proud? "For we are God's workmanship, created in Christ Jesus to do good works, which God prepared in advance for us to do" (Ephesians 2:10).

Use this children's song as a tool to evaluate, before the Lord and with His help, how you and your family are doing. Do you identify and remove hazardous situations, ideas, worldviews, and habits from your lives as promptly as you would a foreign object from your mouth?

So be careful, little eyes, what you see,

So be careful, little eyes, what you see,

For Your Father up above is looking down in love

So be careful, little eyes, what you see.

Being a Righteous Judge

The sounds from the basement tell me that once again the children are having difficulty getting along. I am sorely tempted to either ignore the situation or get angry and yell. But after a deep breath, I realize both responses come from my own human selfishness. I want our children to be perfect now, and I don't want to continually interrupt my day to train and disciple them properly. I also realize that my human responses won't please God, for He wants each parent to be a righteous judge.

We are often called on to be the arbiters of disagreements within our family, which means understanding (sometimes discovering) the truth about what has occurred, listening to the witnesses directly involved, asking the necessary questions, deciding the guilt or innocence of each party involved, and determining a truthful, just, and fair sentence. Sounds like a lot of work! Just this once, Lord, can't I ignore the bickering and finishing mopping the kitchen floor before the water turns cold?

One of God's attributes is that He is a holy and righteous Judge. "His works are perfect, and all his ways are just. A faithful God who does no wrong, upright and just is he" (Deuteronomy 32:4). As a judge, God is totally committed to being fair, impartial, and to bringing the truth to light. Since we as Christian parents desire to be conformed to His image more each day, we need to understand the type of judge He is and grow in our ability to represent Him accurately to our children.

The book of Proverbs is an excellent place to begin learning about God's way of parenting. The first chapter says, "The proverbs of Solomon, son of David, king of Israel: for attaining wisdom and discipline, for understanding words of insight; for acquiring a disciplined and prudent life, doing what is right and just and fair; for giving prudence to the simple, knowledge and discretion to the young" (Proverbs 1:1-4). This is an excellent description of what we need to learn as parents and what we want to convey as truth to the next generation.

Here are some of the truths God has been teaching Steve and me through the years about being righteous judges in our home:

1. Pray for patience, guidance, and discernment whenever we need to enter our family court room. "For the Lord gives wisdom and from his mouth come knowledge and understanding...for he guards the course of the just and protects the way of his faithful ones. Then you will understand what is right and just and fair—every good path" (Proverbs 2:6, 8, 9).

2. Consider carefully and thoughtfully how we should proceed (most often that means thinking before we open our mouths). "The heart of the righteous weighs its answers, but the mouth of the wicked gushes evil" (Proverbs 15:28).

3. Intervene as soon as we realize a dispute has broken out between the children, rather than waiting until the situation is out of control. "Starting a quarrel is like breaching a dam; so drop the matter before a dispute breaks out" (Proverbs 17:14).

4. Ask each child involved, one at a time, for his or her viewpoint on the incident. Each child should be able to share without interruption. Listen thoughtfully and respectfully to all sides, and make no statement until you have heard and cross-examined all parties. "The first to present his case seems right, till another comes forward and questions him" (Proverbs 18:17).

5. Try to be as objective and calm as possible. Do not assume that your son was too harsh until you know that for sure. Do not assume that the baby of the family was innocent merely because he or she is the youngest. Realize that the child you saw or heard lash out verbally or physically may have been responding to another child's subtle instigations that you didn't see or hear. "To show partiality in judging is not good" (Proverbs 24:23).

6. Don't allow your children to excuse their actions by saying "I was just kidding!" The Bible says that "like a madman shooting firebrands (sticks of burning wood) or deadly arrows is a man who deceives his neighbor and says, 'I was only joking!'" (Proverbs 26:18-19).

7. After hearing all sides, you can deliver your verdict of guilt or innocence. Carefully decide which infractions or sins fall to each child involved. One child may be ninety percent wrong while another child is only ten percent at fault. But each should be held responsible for his or her portion of the disagreement—no more and no less. (And don't forget to praise the things that were handled well.) Remember that "acquitting the guilty and condemning the innocent—the Lord detests them both" (Proverbs 17:15).

8. Then, based on individual guilt or innocence, you must decide, with God's wisdom, what consequences each child should bear. Consequences should address the children's heart attitudes, not just their outward behavior, and may consist of further instruction, opportunities to practice correct responses, sincere apologies, reparation for damages done, penalties, disciplines, or punishments, and/or removal of family benefits or privileges.

9. Conclude by stating clearly what you expect from your child in the future. Pray with and for the children involved, and remind them not to keep accounts—what happened is in the past and should not be dredged up again.

Knowing that the kitchen floor is less important in the long run than the character of my children, I put down the mop and head downstairs, praying for wisdom. I know sometime they will be grown and gone, and God will be in charge of their character growth. Maybe by taking care of some little sins today, I can spare them bigger life consequences later.

Satin or Denim?

Gorgeous fabric! Cotton prints for quilting in all colors of the rainbow, snuggly flannels for winter pajamas, and ivory lace for tablecloths at family dinners.

Satin is a shimmery material, soft to the hand, and is used for special occasions like weddings or proms. It cannot take much wear or it will tear. Denim, on the other, is tightly woven and sturdy. This fabric is for every day. Dress it down with boots and a plaid shirt or glam it up with diamonds and heels.

All this talk of fabric reminds me of our faith as women. Some people's faith remains like a beaded party dress protectively wrapped in plastic to be worn only occasionally. It is just too special and fragile for routine use on week days. But I think that faith should be like denim. Sit on the floor in jeans or work in the garden; if it gets dirty, that's okay; go hiking in denim or attend a play.

Now I need Jesus every minute of each day. So do you, I imagine. That kind of continual use requires a strong and serviceable faith that can go anywhere.

In Acts 17:11, 12 we read about the new faith of the people in the city of Berea. "Now these [Bereans] were more noble-minded than those in Thessalonica, for they received the word with great eagerness, examining the Scriptures daily to see whether these things were so. Therefore many of them believed."

These Bereans heard the teaching of Paul and Silas in the synagogues and were considered more excellent than the people of Thessalonia. They deliberately and readily received what Paul taught. And they scrutinized and carefully investigated every day how what was taught lined up with the words of the Old Testament.

We need to take the time (or carve it out) each day to become increasingly familiar with the Bible. What does it say that I need to keep close to my mind and heart today? Use your faith frequently, for faith, like denim, is strong and able to be used day after day.

Is your faith like satin or denim?

A Praiseworthy Arizona Trip

"But now ask the beasts, and let them teach you; and the birds of the heavens, and let them tell you. Or speak to the earth, and let it teach you; and let the fish of the sea declare to you. Who among all these does not know that the hand of the LORD has done this?" Job 12:7-9

Steve and I recently had the opportunity to drive from Denver, CO to Phoenix, AZ. Of course, we love Colorado as this state has been our home since we married in 1975. For six of those years we were in two other states, but both times we scurried back to Colorado as fast as we could.

What an opportunity to praise God on this trip!

We spent the first night in Albuquerque, NM just as the sun was sinking opposite the Sandia Mountains where they sit just east of the city. Such amazing color at that time of day! The word *sandia* is Spanish for "watermelon," almost that same rosy color of the mountains.

Sometime after Albuquerque we notice a solitary, snow-covered peak on the western horizon. As we got drove closer it reminded us of our Pikes Peak outside Colorado Springs, CO. But this peak did not look to be part of an extensive range, but sat almost by itself. This was Humphreys Peak, the tallest peak in Arizona at over 12,600 feet high. It is part of the San Francisco Peaks range in the Coconino National Forest. Lord, can You see this beauty? "For the Lord is a great God and a great King above all gods, in whose hands are the depths of the earth, and the peaks of the mountains are His also" (Psalm 95:3, 4).

Speaking of the depths of the earth, we could have taken the turn-off for the Grand Canyon. *Answers in Genesis* says, "The Grand Canyon is a testament to the amazing power of a lot of water over a little time (and a testament to the God who made this happen)." No time to go north this trip. Hopefully, we will be back!

Discovering Flagstaff was a joy! At seven thousand feet in elevation, it was even higher than our home in Denver. Snow remained on the north-facing slopes, the air was crisp, and smelled of pine. Ponderosa pine trees were everywhere! It reminded us of Conifer, CO in the foothills outside Denver! Who knew there was a place like Colorado in Arizona no less! Later we found out that the town is located in the largest contiguous Ponderosa pine forest in the world! How glorious! Perhaps if we had lowered the window we could have heard singing. "Let the field exult, and all that is in it. Then all the trees of the forest will sing for joy" (Psalm 96:12).

South of Flagstaff we saw highway signs that indicated elk crossings. Awesome, but we didn't catch a glimpse of these magnificant creatures. Then there were some deer crossing signs, but no sight of any of them. Lastly, we almost drove off the road laughing when we saw the signs for--burro crossings! (What?) Not so magnificent but necessary, useful animals.

Between Flagstaff and Sedona we descended about 4,500 feet from pine trees to cacti and Black Canyon City to our east. First, there are a few scattered saguaro cacti and then they are simply everywhere! The saguaro cactus blossom is the state flower of Arizona. "The wilderness and the desert will be glad, and the Arabah will rejoice and blossom; like the crocus" (Isaiah 35:1).

Then we arrived in Phoenix where the sunsets are something amazing to behold. "The heavens are telling of the glory of God; and their expanse is declaring the work of His hands" (Psalm 19:1).

Such a trip to praise the Lord! "Through him all things were made; without him nothing was made that has been made" (John 1:3).

But If Not...

Three little words. A message was sent to London during the summer of 1940. What could it mean?

To the British people familiar with the King James translation of the Bible, it would have instantly brought to mind the book of Daniel and what happened at the fiery furnace. Three of Daniel's friends had been commanded to bow down and worship a ninety-foot-high image of King Nebuchadnezzar of Babylon. But these courageous men had been well-taught from childhood. They knew what God had told their forefathers, "I am the LORD thy God...Thou shalt have no other gods before me. Thou shalt not make...any graven [carved] image: Thou shalt not bow down thyself to them, nor serve them." (Exodus 20:2-5 KJV)

So they refused to bow. The punishment for such disrespect and outright rebellion was to be immediately executed by being thrown into a super-heated furnace.

The men famously replied, "If it be so, our God whom we serve is able to deliver us from the burning fiery furnace, and he will deliver us out of thine hand, O king. But if not, be it known unto thee, O king, that we will not serve thy gods, nor worship the golden image which thou has set up." (Daniel 3:17-18 KJV)

Did you see it? "But if not."

Around 350,000 mostly British troops were desperately trapped near Dunkirk, France. It appeared they were going to be massacred by German soldiers. It was unlikely they could be rescued in time. This was when the three-word message went out, meaning if we are rescued, terrific, but if we are not rescued, that will be okay.

The rest of the story. For some reason, the German troops didn't move for several days. In the meantime, word went out to small boats, commercial vessels, and anything that could float, to start evacuating the troops across the English Channel. What became known as the Miracle at Dunkirk, moved 338,000 Allied troops out of harm's way.

How amazing that three words from Scripture conveyed a much bigger communication!

The Glad Game

Pollyanna: Well, that's the game, you know.
Nancy: What game?

Pollyanna: The "Glad Game." Father taught me it.

Nancy: What is it?

Pollyanna: It started when I wanted a doll. And Father had written asking for one from the charity people, but when it came, there were just some crutches.

Nancy: Crutches?

Pollyanna: Yes, you know. And the game is to find something to be glad about in everything.

Nancy: How can you be glad about having crutches if you

wanted a doll?

Pollyanna: Ah hah! You're glad because you don't need them!

Today's "to do" list: Laundry (still, again, and always). Feed the dog (9 years of dog ownership x 365 days in a year x 2 meals a day = 6,570 pug meals). Shop for dinner (only right now I can't think of a single dinner I have prepared in 34 years of marriage). Drop off/pick up books at the library (note to self: find the library books first). Finish writing an article that is due today (how about starting earlier for a change?). Pack for a trip to California (to bring my laptop or not to bring my laptop). Prepare the Bible study materials for the lesson I have to teach the day after I get back (where are we again?). There, that should about cover everything. Routine, boring routine, a disheartening focus on what has to be done.

When I catch myself sighing about my lot in life, I know it is time for an attitude adjustment. Instead of a complaining woman, I want to be a godly wife and mother who demonstrates a spirit of gratefulness. So God reminds me to play the Glad Game.

Lord, thank You for providing us with a washer and dryer that work—and a basement to put them in. Thank You for the electricity to run the machines, hot water, and detergent to get the sheets and towels clean. Thank You for each of the six people in this home. Thank You that our children are old enough to be responsible for their own appearance and apparel.

Lord, thank You for bringing Penny the pug into our lives. Whatever did we do before we had her? Thank You for how she adorably tilts her head from side to side when we talk to her. Thank You that she is always right by our sides or on our laps, casually draped over the newspaper, books, and important papers we are trying to read. All she wants to do is be with her people. She loves carrots, can take the lid off a water bottle, takes up hardly any space at all, and loves rides. Thank You for her faithful companionship.

About dinnertime, Lord: thank You that You have provided my husband Steve with a well-paying job that provides for what we need—and even what we want! Thank You for grocery stores filled with an amazing variety of dinner options. Thank You for a stove that works, and pots and pans with which to prepare a meal. Thank You for the refrigerator that keeps the lettuce from wilting and the milk from spoiling. Thank You for family members who are a pleasure to cook for, willing to help in the kitchen, and compliment the meal. It truly would be no fun to cook for just me.

Thank You, Lord, for books, books, and more books. Thank You for authors who get their ideas from You and then commit those ideas to paper. Thanks for free public libraries (and Benjamin Franklin, who started the idea). Thank You for all the places I have visited in library books, all the beautiful landscapes I have experienced, and all the skills I have acquired through books.

Thank You for giving me an amazing love for words! Thank You for the privilege to write these words down so that others may be encouraged. Thank You, too for deadlines, because without them I would rarely get the ideas out of my head, squeezed down to my fingers, and out onto paper.

Thank You for the planned trip to California. Only You know my heart's desire to travel—not all the time, but often enough. Thank You that my family is willing to do without me for several days. Thank You that I can visit family members, that we can share meals and an enchanting American castle, and that I can tell each one "I love you" one more time.

Mostly, thank You for the incredible gifts of the Bible and Jesus, my Redeemer! It is an amazing privilege to read, study, and teach the life-giving Word to other moms and daughters! Once I get started studying, You are so very faithful to give me so many insights. Thank You for the women You bring across my path whose hearts are turned toward You. Thank You for the friendships that have developed around the study of Your Word!

Today's "to do" list: adjust my attitude to one of gratefulness—check!

Standing with Puddleglum

> "One word, Ma'am," he said, coming back from the fire; limping, because of the pain. "One word. All you've been saying is quite right, I shouldn't wonder. I'm a chap who always liked to know the worst and then put the best face I can on it. So I won't deny any of what you said."

The speaker in the above quote is dearest Puddleglum from the C.S. Lewis book *The Silver Chair*. Puddleglum is a Marsh-wiggle and he is deep underground in the dark realm of the Lady of the Green Kirtle. He and his young friends are becoming more and more bewitched as the lady speaks to them soothingly, has music that lulls the senses, and casts a green smoke at them causing them to be deceived. They were forgetting that there was a land on the surface called the Sunlit Lands or Overland where a majestic lion named Aslan ruled in a kingdom called Narnia. Even Puddleglum was succumbing to her hypnotic spell untill he deliberately stomps on the fire with his bare feet to jolt himself back to reality. Then comes his most amazing and heroic declaration of faith.

> "But there's one more thing to be said, even so. Suppose we have only dreamed, or made up, all those things--trees and grass and sun and moon and stars and Aslan himself. Suppose we have. Then all I can say is that, in that case, the made-up things seem a good deal more important than the real ones. Suppose this black pit of a kingdom of yours is the only world. Well, it strikes me as a pretty poor one. And that's a funny thing, when you come to think of it. We're just babies making up a game, if you're right. But four babies playing a game can make a play-world which licks your real world hollow. That's why I'm going to stand by the play world. I'm on Aslan's side even if there isn't any Aslan to lead it. I'm going to live as like a Narnian as I can even if there isn't any Narnia. So, thanking you kindly for our supper, if these two gentlemen and the young lady are ready, we're leaving your court at once and setting out in the dark to spend our lives looking for Overland. Not that our lives will be very long, I should think; but that's a small loss if the world's as dull a place as you say."

The world we live in often seems dark and evil and far away from the things of God. The world whispers to us--and sometimes shouts--that there is no God, there are no moral absolutes, an individual life has no value, and man (or woman) is the measure of all things. We can be lulled into believing that these ideas are the real ones and that God Himself, moral absolutes of right and wrong, the value of human life, and that God is sovereign are the made-up things.

Along with Puddleglum, I too choose to stand for the truth of God's word in our daily lives. I am on God's side even if some believe there isn't any God to lead it. I am going to live as a Christian even if some people think there is no Christendom. And I will spend the rest of my life looking for the kingdom where God rules and reigns. So thanking you kindly, world, I won't listen to you anymore.

Care to join us? Will you stand with the Marsh-wiggle and me in our pursuit of a rock solid faith here and now?

Commencement

We were so proud to hand that high school diploma to our son Timothy! Years of home schooling culminated in an all-too-short graduation ceremony. Worried that I might cry, I really only felt an overwhelming sense of gratefulness for all that the Lord Jesus Christ had done for us as a family to bring us to this moment in time.

Pictures of Timothy flashed on the large screens: an adorable baby (aren't all babies truly adorable?); a child dressed for a Christmas photo; a young man holding our much-loved pug. Timothy is our third-born child and our second-born son. He was also the second-to-last of our children to finish home schooling and graduate, ready to move on to bigger and better things. That left us with only one more year with Peter, our youngest, before we would be done home schooling for good. (Sigh! Sniff!)

One question we heard frequently from parents was: "Can homeschooling parents grant a diploma to their own child?" Most definitely! The reason is because a diploma certifies that someone (a parent) has designed a particular course of study and another someone (the student) has completed that course of study satisfactorily.

We participated in the graduation ceremony sponsored by Christian Home Educators of Colorado for all four of our children. I tell people that this is a three- to five-hankie event, depending on how many tears! Generally a maximum of twenty students are recognized per ceremony, so there is plenty of time for the parents to confer the diploma, say some special words of blessing over their child, and for the graduates—in cap and gown—to hand their mothers a rose. There is a commencement speaker as well who offers a challenge to the graduating class of young men and women to continue to serve the Lord for all the days of their lives. Three cheers for the graduates!

Perhaps for you, this moment is still future, and it seems enough of a challenge just to get through today's math lesson! But, in the twinkling of an eye, you too will be standing on a stage with your first graduate.

Many things struck me as important that day, but one thing (other than our Timothy) stood out, and that was the example of the parents in the audience. They had begun to home school years before, and were now seeing the fruit of all that effort and prayer. They had not only started this journey, but they had faithfully completed it as well. I was both thankful and humbled to be in the company of such obedient people. Three cheers for the parents!

How incredibly grateful we are to the Lord for calling us to this adventure of home schooling. After twenty years in the trenches, we can truly testify with joy that God has always, in every situation large or small, provided for us in the most faithful and wonderful of ways. Whether it was pencils and paper, curricula, ideas, patience, time, or special instructors, God gave us everything we needed and then some!

As you home school your children this year, remember to think of the bigger picture: what you are doing and why you are doing it. And "may the Lord bless you and keep you; the Lord make his face shine upon you and be gracious to you; the Lord turn his face toward you and give you peace" (Numbers 6:24-26). Three cheers for homeschoolers!

Conquered by Christ

Homeschoolers often talk about conveying a worldview to their children. All parents, whether they realize it or not, share their particular worldview. But as Christians, Steve and I want to pass on a Christian worldview to the next generation. Worldviews are everywhere. Let's practice identifying the following author's worldview, using this popular poem:

Out of the night that covers me,
Black as the Pit from pole to pole,
I thank whatever gods may be
For my unconquerable soul.

In the fell clutch of circumstance
I have not winced nor cried aloud.
Under the bludgeoning of chance
My head is bloody, but unbowed.

Beyond this place of wrath and tears
Looms but the Horror of the shade,
And yet the menace of the years
Finds, and shall find, me unafraid.

It matters not how strait the gate,
How charged with punishments the scroll.
I am the master of my fate:
I am the captain of my soul.

Do you recognize this poem? It is "Invictus," written by William Ernest Henley and published in 1875. *Invictus* is Latin for "unconquerable." Did you spot the clues to Mr. Henley's worldview? He thanks "whatever gods may be." Sounding doubtful that there is really anyone out there, he offers thanks to a pantheon of gods, perhaps resting on Mount Olympus!

Through his words, Mr. Henley paints a mood of all-encompassing darkness, yet proclaims that whatever the circumstances, he has triumphed over them, refusing to let them conquer his soul. The description reminds me of the disobedient child who, sent to sit in the corner, mutters under his breath, "I'm sitting down on the outside, but I'm standing up on the inside!"

He believes that this present life is filled with tears, and then miserably followed by death. Life is dark, senseless, and pointless. The future is threatening, but he says he is not afraid, like a boy whistling in the face of an oncoming storm.

Then in the fourth stanza, he boldly mocks Matthew 7:14, explaining that it does not matter how narrow the gate is [to get to heaven?] or how long his list of deserved punishments is. With a victorious shout, he arrogantly cries that he alone is in control of his future and his soul.

I studied this poem in high school, and have seen it quoted regularly throughout my life. Most people comment how this is a wonderful example of determination, triumph over circumstances, or the amazing resiliency of the human spirit. But I did not introduce this existential poem to our children until they were firmly grounded in the truths of the Christian faith and were ready to analyze and thoughtfully compare other worldviews.

So imagine my delight when, in contrast, I discovered this poem called "Conquered" in my daughter's Christian literature textbook.

> Out of the light that dazzles me,
> Bright as the sun from pole to pole,
> I thank the God I know to be,
> For Christ—the Conqueror of my soul.
>
> Since His the sway of circumstance,
> I would not wince nor cry aloud.
> Under the rule which men call chance,
> My head, with joy, is humbly bowed.
>
> Beyond this place of sin and tears,
> That Life with Him and His the Aid,
> That, spite the menace of the years,
> Keeps, and will keep me, unafraid.
>
> I have no fear though straight the gate;
> He cleared from punishment the scroll.
> Christ is the Master of my fate!
> Christ is the Captain of my soul!

I love this poem! Do you notice the completely different worldview? Written by Dorothea Day, this version—instead of glorifying a humanist perspective—points us to God's grace and our role as joyful servants. And because this teaches a Christian view of the world, this belongs in every homeschooler's library!

Full of light, "Conquered" is the author's celebration of her personal relationship with Christ. She shares that it is Christ who is sovereign over all the events of life, not random chance, and says it is her joy to humbly bow in worship before her Lord. She admits that this life is filled with troubles, but that she faces the future unafraid with Him by her side. The narrow gate is not too narrow for her to find and willingly walk through, since Christ has taken on Himself the punishment for all her sins. Christ is the Lord of both her future and her eternal soul.

The difference between these two worldviews is vast. One worldview, the Christian one, is the wisest foundation for us as families to build upon. The other worldview, which eliminates God, needs to be consistently rejected. Every single day we walk through life and instruct our children in the difference between these two views. Are you skilled in pointing out God's truth to your precious children? Are you also discerning enough to recognize the false and deliberately remove that from your family life and home education? And, lastly, who is the Captain of your soul: you or the Lord Jesus Christ?

Please Show Me a Wonderful Thing, Lord!

"Now when Jesus saw the crowds, he went up on a mountainside and sat down. His disciples came to him, and he began to teach them. He said: 'Blessed are the poor in spirit, for theirs is the kingdom of heaven.'" Matthew 5:1-3

Did you read the verse above or did you skip it to get to the more "important" parts? Oh, don't skip over the words above! God's words are living and active, they are powerful, and forever. The same cannot be said of my words. So spend your time with the words that have eternal significance. But I want to show you how to do that.

As I am studying the Bible, I often ask God to show me a WT -- a wonderful thing! This prayer idea comes from Psalm 119:18 which says, "Open my eyes that I may see wonderful things in your law."

Now, I am not asking for physical sight, but for spiritual insight from God. Please, Lord, reveal a new thought, disclose a new truth, uncover a connection in my thinking that I need to make, or point out where my present thinking is incorrect and needs to be corrected.

So to start any study of the Bible, first pray that God will give you spiritual eyes, then read the verse, passage, or chapter. Slow down and read it again. Observe what the text says and what it doesn't say. Ask yourself about the sentences and the ideas using question words like what, who, when, where, why, and how. This slows you down enough so you can focus.

Ask questions about Matthew 5:1-3 with obvious answers, like: Who is present in these verses? (Jesus, the crowds, and the disciples are present.) Where did He go when He saw the crowds? (He went up on the mountain.) When did His disciples come to Him? (They came to Him after He sat down on the mountain.) What did He begin to do? (He began to teach them.)

Ask questions about the verses for which you may not know the answers, like:

Who is blessed? (I am not sure.) What does it mean to be poor in spirit? (Maybe I can look that up somewhere?) Where is the kingdom of heaven? (Is this answer going to be on a map?) How do you get to be poor of spirit? (I'm not sure?)

Bible study doesn't require a PhD, which is good, because I don't have one of those! But it does require time to read and work through the questions, patience with the process, and a quiet place to be able to think. These three commodities: time, patience, and a quiet place, are difficult to come by in this present world, but not impossible. If you can start small with even five minutes you will begin to grow in your knowledge and understanding of God's words. And you will love the benefits, I promise!

Walk as Children of Light

"[F]or you were formerly darkness, but now you are Light in the Lord; walk as children of Light." Ephesians 5:8

There are certain things which a Christian should have nothing to do with.

As children of light we have no business trifling with spiritual darkness. God already rescued us from the domain of darkness and transferred us to Jesus' kingdom (Colossians 1:13.) There is no way we should want to head back to the bondage of the domain of darkness.

As we homeschooled our children, we often took the opportunity of the dark emphasis of the end of October to work on discussing or memorizing a portion of Deuteronomy 18:9-13. We prayed that their knowledge of the word over time would protect them.

Here is that passage with parentheses to explain the words used. Just read it carefully and slowly. Do you know this and can you share it with your children?

verse 9 "When you enter the land (Canaan) which the LORD your God gives you, you shall not learn to imitate (acquire, observe, celebrate) the detestable (disgusting, abominable things: having to do with unclean things, idols, or wickedness) things of those [Canaanite, heathen] nations.

verse 10 "There shall not be found among you anyone who makes his son or his daughter pass through the fire (any worshipper of the pagan god Molech; see Leviticus 18:21), one who uses divination (witchcraft), one who practices witchcraft (to observe times, practice soothsaying, spiritism, magic, or augury), or one who interprets omens (practices fortune telling), or a sorcerer (a person who claims to have magic powers; a witch or wizard),

verse 11 "or one who casts a spell (one who enchants with a charm or hex to evoke a magical effect), or a medium (one who acts as an intermediary between humans and demonic beings), or a spiritist (one who has a familiar spirit, a demonic servant available to do human commands), or one who calls up the dead (one who pretends to consult dead people).

verse 12 "For whoever does these things is detestable to the LORD; and because of these detestable things the LORD your God will drive (dispossess, destroy, bring to ruin) them [the Canaanites] out before you.

verse 13 "You shall be blameless (complete, whole, entire, sound of mind and body) before the LORD your God.

verse 14 "For those nations, which you shall dispossess, listen to those who practice witchcraft and to diviners (a person who uses special demonic powers to predict future events), but as for you, the LORD your God has not allowed (permitted) you to do so."

What do you observe from these verses? How will observing these words protect you and your children?

Confessions of a Homeschool Mom

I think perhaps it is time for some true confessions (gulp!) It has been an awesome privilege to get to share what was on my heart. All along the way, it has been my desire to share what God has taught our family during the twenty plus years we have been on this home schooling adventure together! I have freely received so much and have wanted to just as freely give back to the next generation of homeschooling families.

Through it all, my highest honor has come from being Steve's wife and Amanda, Jonathan, Timothy, and Peter's mother, as well as being their primary teacher. We haven't published books (until now!) or started a home business, and, no, I don't have a table in the Exhibit Hall at the conference! Thus far there hasn't been the time for those things or, more importantly, the calling from God.

Like you, I have prayed, wept, been undecided about a hundred things, and worried to death that our children would be juvenile delinquents sometime in the next, oh, twenty minutes, and that it would be completely my fault! I have lost sleep, concerned that what we were doing in our home school was too much or maybe not enough. I have thrown teacher's guides across the room in temper and frustration (and repented for my display of anger).

There have been books that we didn't finish—either because we ran out of days in May or the book simply wasn't interesting any longer. Amanda didn't really have a third grade year because we were living in the basement of some friends' house and yet somehow (thank You, God, again!) she did amazingly well on her achievement tests that year (I don't recommend this as standard procedure, by the way)! It took us two years to finish biology in high school and we never even started chemistry. Jonathan skipped junior high altogether, because he was ready and would have been bored stiff if we had kept him in a holding pattern for two years. Timothy and Peter learned everything together until just before Tim's junior year.

We haven't done every math problem on every page, we didn't start history until fifth grade, and we read all sorts of library books —on bugs, volcanoes, and Jupiter—for science in elementary school, but no "school" books until junior high. I have corrected all the work they ever did, generally right on the spot and often upside-down, but I officially graded none of it until high school and then only quizzes and major tests. We only home schooled four days a week when the children were younger, allowing for doctors' appointments, laundry, snuggling more with the baby, or just being a family. We often took off the entire month of December to plan Christmas together. For years we had a required silent reading time every school day after lunch—the children could nap, read, or do something quietly on their own beds for about an hour, while I collapsed, took a nap, or did something fun. We have home schooled in a dedicated school room, in the car, on vacation, while I was sick in bed, at the dining room table, and in the sunny patch on the living room floor! We have continued to home school while the house was up for sale, when Steve lost his job, when we had money and when we had none, when we moved from Colorado to Indiana to Colorado to Texas, and then back to Colorado again, when I was pregnant, when I miscarried, and when I was trusting God completely and when my faith faltered and I was fearful. We have persevered and grieved through the deaths of three grandfathers, two grandmothers, and one great-grandmother.

In summary, we haven't come close to perfection in our home schooling. That is a miserable and disheartening myth—there is no perfect family and there is no perfect way to home school. We have merely asked the Lord to be our Teacher in all things: faith, character, life, and academics. Our prayer has been to be a family that is growing up in the Lord together in the "life laboratory" that is our home and to be a lighthouse to other families about the Truth of Christ Jesus. We have desired to live out the reality of this truth in our daily life and in our "divine appointments" with other people.

It was the Lord who put this calling on our hearts and to have done otherwise would have been disobedient. When He calls His children, He wants us to be available, to show up for work each morning, and do our very best, and He promises to provide all that we each need. God gave our family a verse to hang on to back in 1986 when we first began this amazing journey. I share it with you now, as one humanly imperfect mother who believes in an almighty God: "Let us not become weary in doing good, for at the proper time we will reap a harvest if we do not give up" (Galatians 6:9).

Tips from a Homeschool Veteran

After being a homeschooling family for over twenty years (thank You, Lord!), here are some of the most helpful tips I have collected about surviving this incredible adventure. These are in no particular order.

1. Get ready for your day first thing in the morning.

2. Figure out what's for dinner by mid-morning.

3. Consider a dress standard for your home school—nice clothes make attitudes less sluggish.

4. Put your phones on Do Not Disturb!

5. Have a place for everything, and try to put it back in its place as you go through the day.

6. Simplify meals.

7. Decrease your expectations regarding housework and laundry. Find a balance between trying to maintain a show home and living in one that should be condemned by the health department. Realize that you live here 24/7 (unlike many families who vacate the house), and remember that you are not taking your house or your possessions to heaven—only eternal souls!

8. Remember that the word "home" comes before "school" for a reason! Creating a godly home is the priority.

9. Always try to speak respectfully to and about your husband and your children.

10. Seek out like-minded people—in person or through books, conferences, and online.

11. Write down your reasons for home schooling. Re-read your list often!

12. Provide on-the-job training for your children—teach and demonstrate a task, watch as your child tries it, then correct as needed. Children need to learn life skills like cleaning toilets and doing laundry, and you need the help!

13. Deliberately teach life skills and social skills, in addition to academic skills.

14. Decide to study and learn everything from a Christian per-
    spective so your children can develop their own discernment.

15. Look for evidence of God in every subject, then recognize and
    acknowledge His fingerprints in the world and in every
    school subject.

16. Teach using the 2 Peter 1:5-8 model: develop faith first, then
    personal character, then focus on academic knowledge. Our
    children can study almost anything, but if they don't have a
    solid faith and godly character, they are truly shortchanged.

17. Study great heroes and heroines of the Christian faith to en-
    courage you to follow Christ no matter the cost.

18. Always stop academics in order to teach faith and character—
    correcting a bad attitude is always more important than fin-
    ishing a sample math problem!

19. Don't reinvent the wheel! Use Christian curriculum and teach-
    ers' guides.

20. Know that teachers in public schools do not always do every
    problem on a page, answer every question on the chapter re-
    view, or finish the entire textbook; they carefully select what
    their students most need and teach it as best they can in the
    time allotted.

21. Keep an encouragement book, filled with Scripture verses,
    quotes, and pictures that help you remember why you are a
    Christian woman, wife, mom, and homeschooling teacher.

22. Realize that home schooling is multi-generational. What you
    do today has incredible significance and is shaping a legacy
    for future generations, as long as the Lord wills. (See
    Deuteronomy 4:9.)

23. Understand that God has a plan for parents, in addition to the
    one for our children. He put you together with your children
    because He knew you both needed each other and would
    grow in grace and knowledge together for His glory.

24. Be willing to share with others the things God has taught you.

25. Pray unceasingly, with thanksgiving, expecting God to answer!

All Over Again

In the last twenty years we have grown from a family of four to a family of six, we have lived and home schooled in three states, and we have seen all four of our children graduate from high school. Steve and I have sat at each graduation, holding hands and marveling at all the other parents in attendance who have also "gone the distance," those who did "not become weary in well-doing," those who by the grace of God have completed the assignment given by God.

To have done anything else other than home school these precious children would have been in direct disobedience to what we knew God had called us to do.

We have witnessed God direct the writing of the homeschool law here in Colorado through Christopher Klicka, Treon Goosen, and others. In 1994, we were one of the families that helped to shut down the Congressional switchboard regarding a House bill called H.R. 6. We have called and written our legislators and congressmen and tried to remain vigilant so that home schooling might still be an option for our children's children, if the Lord should tarry.

We have read almost every Christian book about home schooling and tried to put the best bits into practice. We have attended almost twenty home school state conferences—in Indiana, Texas, and Colorado—and countless local support group meetings. I have talked over coffee or on the phone for hours on end with hesitant or struggling moms, encouraging them to trust the Lord with every aspect of their home schooling. I have written for, spoken to, cried with, and prayed over many support groups around the state. I have had the privilege and honor of giving years of conference workshops here in Colorado. I have been part of writing, compiling, and revising a state guide for home schooling that is even bigger than anything the big state of Texas has produced! I have been a support group member, leader, and advisory board member.

Going over the basic K-12 education four times now means I should know something! (Not only do we have intelligent children in home schooling, but also the smartest, best-schooled moms anywhere!) I finally get algebra and (gulp) even like it! We have studied Shakespeare, British literature, martial arts, piano, and ballet. We have gone on educational hunts to discover God in mathematics, science, art, literature, and history. We have dissected four fetal pigs and I have not thrown up. We have been to the library so many times that the librarians know me by name! I have had a Christian education for myself that was far better than anything I could have imagined in the beginning.

Back in 1986, we started our home school adventure with our daughter, who was closely followed by three sons. At the end of May 2006, after watching our youngest, Peter, graduate, I put away my globe and pencil sharpener, at least until there are more Lewises that perhaps I could help educate! Although I feel a little bittersweet about closing the book on this chapter of our lives, I look forward to the next stage of serving my Lord. I figure that my job here on earth is not done until they close the lid of my coffin!

As I look back on the years, my heart overflows with love and gratefulness to God for the marvelous journey He envisioned and designed for us in 1986! Steve and I have fallen more in love with God and with each other, and have seen each of our children fall in love with God and ask Him to be the Boss of their lives. I have so appreciated all the godly men, women, and families who have walked before us and beside us along this path. May God richly bless each and every one of you!

Asked recently if I would do it all over again, knowing what I now know, I responded without hesitation, "In a heartbeat!"

May You Find Joy in the Journey

"There is a wonder and wildness to life."

What amazing lyrics written by Christian singer and songwriter Michael Card. I long to take these words, emblazon them across my life, and make them true each and every day!

In the chorus, he writes, "There is a joy in the journey, there's a light we can love on the way. There is a wonder and wildness to life, and freedom for those who obey."

More than seventy years have taught me many lessons about life. How life is sometimes filled with energy-draining fear, crushing disappointment, overwhelming sadness, and unbearable loss. There are sometimes ho-hum, ordinary days that are nothing noteworthy. (Such days, I believe, are seriously underrated! Now that is another post for another day!) And then there are days of breathtaking joy. Being a Christian, a believer in the Lord Jesus Christ, accentuates the tremendous joy of living, for it creates the solid foundation for building a life of joy.

But looking out over all these days, I want to recognize the joy and the privilege that life truly is. Thank You, Lord, for all the experiences and circumstances of my life. Thank you for breathing life into me. Thank You for loving me, even at my most unlovable.

Michael Card was correct, life is truly wonderful and wild, like standing near a waterfall hearing the thunderous roar of the water and the feeling of invigorating mist on your face. Imagine every sunrise you have witnessed, every surprise you have ever known, add in piles of wiggly puppies, a baby's laughter, the scent of an old-fashioned rose, and the taste of lemonade in the summer. If you roll that all together, you can begin to approximate how astonishing life really is.

My prayer for you as you read this: May you, too, find joy in the journey of your life!